The Cuban Revolution in Crisis

The Cuban Revolution in Crisis

From Managing Socialism to Managing Survival

Frank T. Fitzgerald

Monthly Review Press
New York

Library of Congress Cataloging-in-Publication Data
Fitzgerald, Frank T.
    The Cuban Revolution in crisis : from managing socialism to manag-
ing survival / by Frank T. Fitzgerald
        p. cm.
    Includes bibliographic references.
    ISBN 0-85345-889-8 : $34.00 — ISBN 0-85345-890-1 (pbk.) : $16.00
    1. Social classes—Cuba. 2. Professional employees—Cuba—Political ac-
tivity. 3. Cuba—Politics and government—1959-
    I. Title.
    HN210. Z9. S635 1994   94-11818
    320.97291' 09' 049—dc20   CIP

Monthly Review Press
122 West 27th Street
New York NY 10001

Manufactured in the United States of America
10 9 8 7 6 5 4 3 2 1

For all Cubans who, in these mean times,
continue to struggle for democracy and social justice,
for freedom and egalitarianism—for socialism.

And for my parents, Ted and Alice Fitzgerald,
who struggled through their own mean times
with courage.

Contents

Preface

I have been writing about the Cuban revolution for many years, and several of the topics developed here are ones that I have examined before, especially in my book *Managing Socialism: From Old Cadres to New Professionals in Revolutionary Cuba* (New York: Praeger, 1990).

My research for that book was completed in the mid-1980s. Since then, Cuba and the rest of the world have undergone sweeping changes. Among these, the collapse of Soviet-bloc Communism stands out both for its global consequences and for its impact on Cuba. Like Zeus throwing down a thunderbolt, Communism's collapse hurled the Cuban revolution out of its Olympic refuge in the Soviet bloc; in a flash, the island revolution found itself adrift on Poseidon's stormy seas, with no sure moorings in sight. This cataclysm called my attention once again to the Cuban revolution, and moved me to rethink old topics, to explore new ones, and to extend my interpretations into the present. The result is this new book.

I never could have gathered the information for this study without the many Cuban *compañeros* and *compañeras* who generously engaged in long and, for me, fruitful discussions, or without the many librarians at the College of Saint Rose, State University of New York at Albany, New York State Library, University of Massachusetts at Amherst, University of Pittsburgh, United Nations, and the Center for Cuban Studies, who helped me find what I needed, even when I was not sure what that was. I thank them all.

Writing this book forced me to grapple with the published or unpublished questions of several scholars. I am especially grateful to Linda Fuller, James Cockcroft, Arthur MacEwan, and James Petras for understanding, appreciating, and intelligently criticizing my views. I think they will recognize where I have addressed their questions, even when they disagree with my answers.

Nothing facilitates an author's work like an intelligent, knowledgeable, encouraging, and patient editor, behind whose kindly prodding the author, even though he has no evidence, imagines a fearful mass of hysteria, roiling more as each deadline passes. My editor, Ethan Young, had each of these qualities and this effect. I thank him for it all, and for his good humor throughout.

As usual, my wife, Pamela M. Robèrt, has been a fount of encouragement and good company. Despite her own heavy load and impressive accomplishments, she provided me, once again, with an emotional atmosphere and an occasional *mae geri* to expedite my work. I thank her profusely.

I also thank my fellow editors at *Science & Society*, but especially David Laibman, for respecting my self-declared sabbatical as I worked on this book.

Lastly, the usual caveat: Anything wrong with the facts or interpretations that follow is my fault alone.

Chapter 1
Introduction: Roots of the Crisis

Cuba in the 1990s abounds with signs of crisis. Crop yields fall for lack of fertilizers, weed killers, fuel, and parts for irrigation pumps. Scarcities idle harvesting, lifting, loading, and moving equipment; crops sometimes mature only to rot in the field. Factories close due to lack of fuel and raw materials.

Hospital equipment, without spare parts, goes unrepaired. Medical doctors, lacking medicines, anxiously seek herbal cures. Newspapers and magazines are in short supply: no paper. Lack of gas, oil, batteries, and tires cripples buses, trucks, and cars. Stores, offices, and homes darken as electrical output falters. Cooking gas is available for only a few hours each morning and evening.

Food, tightly rationed, is in short supply and lacks variety. Children over seven years old are no longer guaranteed a quart of milk per day. Forced vegetarianism becomes the norm as animal products grow scarcer. A mysterious epidemic—over 50,000 diagnosed cases—of nerve damage and vision loss is attributed, in part, to widespread vitamin deficiencies.

In September 1990, President Fidel Castro declared that Cuba had entered a "special period in time of peace." The term derives from Cuba's plans, ready for many years, to survive a "special period" of military aggression and total naval blockade of the island by the United States. And in fact this peacetime crisis approaches the severity of war; it is revolutionary Cuba's worst crisis ever.

Although factors within Cuba have contributed to it and

recent U.S. policy has worsened it, Cuba's current special period is the result, first and foremost, of the collapse of Soviet-bloc communism.

Cuba began to integrate economically with the Soviet bloc in the early 1970s. In 1972, Cuba joined the Council for Mutual Economic Assistance (CMEA, the former Soviet bloc's common market), which would supply the country with favorable trade arrangements and increasing amounts of development assistance. Starting in 1976, Cuba's five-year economic plans were coordinated with those of the other CMEA countries, and the price of Cuban sugar exports to the Soviet Union was indexed to the price of Soviet oil exports to Cuba. Over time, partly because of this and other beneficial agreements, Cuban trade moved away from the capitalist economies and toward the socialist ones.

In the early 1970s, Cuba concentrated about 65 percent of the value of its total trade turnover (imports plus exports) with the socialist economies; by 1988—just before the downfall of the Communist regimes of Eastern Europe, the disbanding of the CMEA, and the disintegration of the Soviet Union itself—the socialist economies accounted for about 87 percent of the total value of Cuba's foreign trade.

As Soviet-bloc communism proceeded to collapse, Cuba's favorable CMEA trade agreements quickly unraveled. Cuba's CMEA trading partners began supplying fewer commodities and demanding payment in hard currency. By 1990, Cuba was suffering from falling imports of grains, foodstuffs, spare parts, fuels, fertilizers, and other vital materials. Between 1989 and 1992, Cuba's annual oil imports from Russia dropped from 13.3 to 1.8 million tons; fertilizers, from 1.3 to .25 million tons; animal feed, from 1.6 to .45 million tons. In just these few years, Cuba's total trade with the former CMEA countries fell an astounding 93 percent, and Cuban national income plummeted almost 45 percent.[1] The Cuban economy was in shock. The Cuban revolution was in crisis.

As soon as this crisis erupted, some Cuban exiles in the United States began to proclaim that the revolution's demise was imminent. As early as late 1989, cars in Miami's Cuban-American neighborhoods began sporting bumper stickers reading, "Next Year in Havana." These have begun to tatter by now, but the plans of some to return to Cuba have continued apace. Formerly propertied exiles have developed a registry to formally stake claim to the lands, houses, and businesses they once left behind in Cuba and soon hoped to regain. Exiles have flooded McDonald's, the leading U.S. fast-food chain, with applications for the franchise to Havana's first "Golden Arches." Most ominously, as U.S. authorities have looked the other way, several Cuban exile paramilitary groups have reestablished training camps in the Florida Everglades in preparation for an eventual invasion of Cuba.

By far the most noted Cuban exile to anticipate the revolution's end has been Jorge Mas Canosa, wealthy Miami businessman and chair of the Cuban American National Foundation (CANF).[2] Mas Canosa has both claimed and disclaimed an interest in personally replacing Fidel Castro as president of Cuba. His foundation has already drafted a new "democratic" constitution and set up a "blue ribbon commission" to plan and line up investors for a post-Castro, capitalist Cuba. Both ventures have brought together rich Cuban exiles, U.S. officials, and U.S. corporate managers to plan Cuba's capitalist and "democratic" future—without regard for the desires of the island's citizens.

Mas Canosa has been a front man for U.S. policy toward Cuba since the early years of Ronald Reagan's presidency. Mas Canosa participated in the U.S.-sponsored Bay of Pigs invasion in 1961, and was associated thereafter with numerous operatives and operations of the U.S. Central Intelligence Agency; but he became a prominent, influential public figure only after 1980. In that year, at the behest of Richard Allen, CIA veteran and Reagan's national security advisor, Mas Canosa helped create CANF, a well-heeled "educational" organization with lobbying and political campaign financing arms. Since 1982, when the Reagan administration set up the National Endowment for Democracy (NED) to fund private promoters of "democracy" around the world, the United States has funneled over $1 million in NED funds to projects and persons connected with Mas Canosa's CANF.

A creature of U.S. policy, Mas Canosa, in turn, has increasingly helped to shape that policy. He was a major force, for example, behind the 1992 passage of the so-called Cuban Democracy Act (CDA), which he reportedly drafted in part. This opportunistic bill sought to weaken the Cuban revolution by deepening the crisis it faced as Soviet-bloc communism collapsed. Politically, the act tightened restrictions and increased penalties against U.S. citizens who travel to Cuba, authorized Washington to encourage and finance dissidents in Cuba, and advocated improving telephone and mail service between the United States and Cuba—so long as the latter gained no economic benefit—as a way of exciting popular dissatisfaction with economic conditions in the country. Economically, the bill authorized the seizure of any ship entering U.S. waters within 180 days of docking in Cuba and made it illegal for foreign subsidiaries of U.S. corporations to trade with Cuba.

This latter and central provision of the CDA tightened the U.S. blockade of Cuba, which had been put into place piece by piece in the early 1960s and consolidated under the Trading with the Enemy Act in 1963. During that period, U.S. officials often publicly justified the blockade as a way of discouraging the Soviets or Cubans from expanding politically and militarily in the Western hemisphere. Among themselves, however, U.S. officials typically discussed the blockade as a way toward either preventing Cuba from becoming a socialist economic showcase or provoking political discontent on the island.[3] The collapse of Soviet-bloc Communism undermined all but the last of these rationales. Consequently, CDA supporters could appeal to nothing more noble than their own hatred of Cuba's revolutionary regime, a hatred they wanted to spread throughout the Cuban population.

The U.S. blockade always included extensive efforts to discourage third countries from doing business with Cuba, and originally it kept U.S. citizens and corporations from trading with Cuba at all. Beginning in 1975, however, foreign subsidiaries of U.S. companies were allowed to engage in trade with Cuba if that trade was first licensed by the U.S. Treasury Department. In 1988, just before the collapse of Soviet-bloc communism, the total value of such licensed trade stood at $246 million, and Cuba exported more to U.S. subsidiaries than it imported from them. By 1991, however, the value of this trade had jumped to $718 million; over 53 percent of this amount was accounted for by Cuban imports, and over 90 percent of these imports were foodstuffs. The Cuban revolution was riding out its crisis, in part, with the help of food imported from U.S. subsidiaries. Supporters of the CDA sought to end this reprieve; under their banner of "democracy," they were willing to further sacrifice the food supply of the Cuban people.

Even though the inhumanity of the CDA was ignored, considerable controversy surfaced in the congressional hearings leading up to its passage. Two pragmatic criticisms were leveled at the CDA. On the one hand, it was suggested that further squeezing the Cuban economy would be counterproductive (given the unquestioned, strategic goals of U.S. policy): It would help consolidate Cuba's revolutionary regime, rather than subverting it, by lending credence to claims that the island was under imperialist attack. On the other hand, it was suggested that outlawing the Cuban trade of U.S. corporate subsidiaries would infringe on the sovereignty of the countries where they were located and would anger some of Washington's closest allies. This latter was also the reason originally given by the administration of George Bush for opposing the CDA. But when candidate Bill Clinton went to Miami to meet with Mas Canosa, to speak publicly in favor of the CDA, and to collect at least $275,000 in campaign contributions, Bush quickly changed his mind. He signed the CDA into law in October 1992.

The CDA is in place, but its introduction helped to energize a struggle over U.S. policy toward Cuba that shows no signs of abating. The inhumanity of the CDA has given rise to increasing public opposition to U.S. policy toward Cuba in general and to the U.S. economic blockade in particular, as a growing movement has emerged to lobby against the blockade and to subvert it by sending material aid directly to Cuba.

Even growing numbers of Cubans in the United States—many of whom now think of themselves as immigrants rather than exiles, intending to stay rather than return to Cuba—now consider Cuba's future an issue for Cubans on the island rather than for themselves to decide. Many of these Cuban-Americans are openly pressuring to end the U.S. blockade out of concern for the health and safety of their families and friends in Cuba.

At the start of his second year in office, it remains to be seen how President Clinton will respond to these pressures and counterpressures. If the grassroots movement gains sufficient strength, or if U.S. corporations, some of whom opposed the CDA, were to conclude that their interests would be better served by ending the blockade, Clinton could change direction. So far the administration has held firm to established policy. But the pressure—from all directions—is likely to increase.

The Promise of This Book

As this political controversy goes on, Fidel Castro will continue to serve as the Cuban revolution's lightning rod, attracting many of the invectives (and occasional accolades) that come its way. Politicians and pundits in this country frequently speak of Castro's Cuba, as if revolutionary Cuba were his alone. But this only points up the inadequacy of the "elite/mass" perspective from which Cuba is commonly viewed. In this perspective, analogous to the "Kremlin-watching" perspective that long dominated Soviet studies, Cuba's revolutionary leadership is an all-powerful elite in control of a virtually powerless and therefore politically irrelevant mass. Scholars with this perspective have focused disproportionately on Cuba's top leaders, and have paid scant attention to the political importance of the intermediate and lower levels of Cuban society.

By contrast, this book—essentially a work of political sociology that focuses on the relationship between social stratification and politics broadly conceived—examines major changes at the intermediate level of Cuban society, which have been brought about by and have in turn influenced the Cuban revolutionary process. Specifically, this work focuses on the rise and decline of different types of intermediate-level social actors, and on patterns of conflict and cooperation between these sectors, the revolutionary leadership, and workers. First, it examines the revolution's initially poor skill profile, which arose in part from the exodus of the country's prerevolutionary intermediate strata. Second, it explores the conditions that spurred the rise and subsequent decline of what I call "old (political) cadres," who in the 1960s entered intermediate-level occupations on the basis of political rather than educational credentials. Third, it traces the emergence of what I call the "new professionals," who largely after 1970 entered these same types of occupations on the basis of educational credentials and presumed expertise.

This approach is born of important theoretical and empirical considerations. First, if the emphasis on the personage Fidel Castro was ever useful, it will not continue to be for long. Fidel Castro has intimated that he will retire within five years (in 1998, the end of his current term in office), if Cuba has by then resolved its current crisis.[4] Whether this comes to pass or not, however, Castro's days as the revolution's preeminent leader are numbered. If for no other reason than age, he eventually must step down. It is, consequently, now more than ever necessary to look beyond Castro and the aging group of leaders that he has headed since the revolution's start.

In this regard, it is particularly important to pay attention to Cuba's new professionals. Rapidly expanding in number and influence since the 1970s, and especially after 1975, more and more new professionals have occupied critical intermediate-level positions and have become an important sociopolitical force in Cuban society. Furthermore, it is from among these new professionals that Cuba's new leaders already are emerging. Although Cuba scholars have paid insufficient attention to these new professionals,[5] as this study will demonstrate, it is not possible to adequately comprehend the contours of stratification or the conflicts of politics in revolutionary Cuba without recognizing the importance of these new social actors.

Moreover, even though Cuba's current crisis was largely induced by external events, it cannot be fully understood without focusing on the new professionals. On the one hand, the revolution's current leadership, in trying to find ways out of this crisis, has placed enormous stock in the creativity and skills of the new professionals. The leadership, for example, has called upon new professional scientists to develop products that Cuba can sell competitively on the world capitalist market. On the other hand, revolutionary Cuba's current crisis also has a political dynamic which involves all Cubans, but especially the new professionals. As the most educated of Cubans, the new professionals have led the call for greater political openness in determining the way out of the current crisis and toward a continuation of the revolution. Thus, although it is possible to understand the origins of the current crisis in Cuba without attending to the new professionals, they must be focused on to understand Cuba's economic and political future.

There are also important theoretical reasons to look beyond Cuba's most prominent leaders. Ultimate policy decisions in Cuba, of course, are made by the top revolutionary leadership. But, as a critic of the Kremlin-centered perspective in Soviet studies once underscored, actors from other social levels have commonly intervened "in the phase of deliberation prior to the formal making of final decisions" and again "in the period of implementing such decisions."[6] The way to move beyond the elite/mass perspective, therefore, is to widen our focus of attention to bring these moments of the decision-making process into view.

Even if it could be shown for revolutionary Cuba that intermediate actors and workers typically had little or no say in pre-decision-making discussions, they would necessarily play an important role in post-decision-making implementation. As the direct producers of economic goods and services, in fact, workers possess ultimate responsibility for the successful implementation of many types of economic decisions. And both workers and intermediate actors, at the very least, can always execute or block, expedite or delay, abide by or distort, the implementation of leadership decisions. Understanding what is happening in Cuba at any point, as opposed to simply what the leadership has decided should happen, therefore requires attending to the critical role that both intermediate actors and workers play in implementing higher decisions.

Furthermore, except in peculiar circumstances, one would not expect decision-making power to be so concentrated in the hands of top leaders that they alone would participate in pre-decision-making discussions. Intermediate actors, for example, are likely to be called upon by leaders to take part in the pre-decision-making phase, if for no reason other than that they possess relevant information, knowledge, or skills. The degree to which intermediate actors actually influence leadership decisions, of course, is likely to vary widely, from issue to issue, within the same society from time to time, from society to society—but the influence of these actors is only rarely likely to be absent altogether.

Again, the same holds for workers. In fact, there are at least two structural reasons to expect that workers in socialist systems (such as Cuba has had, and officially still upholds) will commonly participate and wield some influence in pre-decision-making discussions. First, in socialist systems the line that separates the private and public spheres is radically different from that in capitalist systems. State ownership of the major means of production results in political and economic organizations, as well as organizational leadership groups, being less officially differentiated from one another than they are, at least formally, in capitalist systems.

Therefore, what are commonly considered private economic issues under capitalism quickly become public issues in a socialist system. Issues such as wage levels, incentive systems, even utilization of the economic surplus, which under capitalism are commonly segregated into the private or nonpolitical sphere, are typically turned into fully political issues in socialist systems.

As a result, it is difficult, if not impossible, for socialist leaders to deny their share of responsibility for unpopular economic policies or results, and even socialist workers concerned solely with "economistic" issues of wages and benefits are often brought into direct political conflict with the leadership. If workers are not allowed some degree of pre-decision-making participation, or if their expectations are not accommodated to some extent, the consequences are likely to be politically disruptive. Socialist leaders who recognize this are likely to favor some measure of worker participation, and commonly will at least take note of worker expectations in their policy calculations.

Second, socialist systems guarantee something very close to full employment. In this, they differ qualitatively from capitalist systems, which require a surfeit of labor to keep workers afraid for their jobs, and thus subservient and disciplined. This structural difference, moreover, is not simply economic but profoundly political. In socialist systems, what Max Weber once dubbed the "whip of hunger" no longer operates with full force, and productive effort must be elicited from workers through other means. Without effective mechanisms to replace the pressures of the capitalist labor market, socialist systems can be expected to face continual productivity crises which in themselves are likely to result in political problems. The fact that socialist government leaders cannot resort to unemployment to back up their attempt to elicit productive effort gives workers considerable political leverage. This they commonly express through noncooperation with economic goals, policies, and norms, unless they are allowed at least minimal participation in decision-making.

To deal with these structural realities, socialist government leaders have two types of choices. They can either opt for coercion—a short-run solution that always entails long-run problems—or for a program that in some measure enlists workers with consumer goods, social services, political exhortation, and worker participation. The last in part accounts for the peculiar institutional structure of socialist societies, which often places great emphasis on mechanisms of mass participation. Those who scoff at such mechanisms as only ritualistic have to be asked why so much energy is spent on mere window dressing. Surely such mechanisms signal the need for leaders to elicit voluntary cooperation from labor that cannot easily be kept focused on economistic demands and that is no longer threatened by the whip of hunger.

These, then, are some of the more important empirical and theoretical justifications for the approach of this book. Again, this book will focus on major changes at the intermediate level of Cuban society over the course of the revolution. This focus on the changing contours of stratification and the multisided conflicts of politics, promises a deeper understanding of the Cuban revolution's course, current crisis, and possible future.

Terms and Concepts

The terms and concepts used in the social sciences are seldom innocent. They commonly carry, at the very least, the connotations of their origins. The social sciences developed in an attempt to comprehend the transition from feudalism to capitalism and the subsequent trajectory of the latter, and social science terminology is filled with meanings associated with these processes. A danger therefore exists that, when applied to other processes like the Cuban revolutionary process discussed here, such terms and concepts will obscure more than they illuminate, distort more than they clarify.

Here this problem arises most obviously with the term "profession." As Eliot Friedson has emphasized, this term has carried two very different meanings, which often have been confused.[7] In its strong sense, "profession" refers to a limited number of occupations whose incumbents successfully organize themselves, develop an exclusive identity, and claim esoteric status for their knowledge and skills, in order to gain advantages of prestige, income, and shelter from market competition. It is "profession" in this strong sense that has drawn attention from Friedson and other sociologists concerned with the pursuit of professionalization and professional authority by certain occupations in developed capitalist societies.

In its weak sense, however, "profession" refers to a broad stratum of quite varied intermediate-level occupations that are distinguished from other occupations simply by the higher level of education they require. In this weak sense, professions exist in all types of societies that have reached a level of economic development that requires advanced qualifications through specialized education. In Cuba, entry into this intermediate-level stratum of occupations has come to require at least a secondary school degree. It is professions in this weak sense that concern us here.

The reader should note that the social actors referred to here as "new professionals" could also be called new mental workers, new technicians, new managers, new specialists, or a variety of other names. All of these categories call attention to certain characteristics and distract from other aspects of the whole occupational stratum. For many readers, for example, new mental workers might signify primarily individuals directly involved in production, and it might distract attention from, say, university professors. I chose the name "new professionals" to draw attention to the fact that these social actors enter intermediate-level occupations on the basis of presumed expertise as judged by their educational credentials. Several other terms that I use throughout this book, such as "revolutionary leadership," "intermediate-level occupations," "political cadres," and "old cadres," fortunately do not present the same difficulties as "new professionals" and simply require formal definition.

The revolutionary leadership is that relatively small number of top-level leaders who, although they may do much else besides, make the fundamental policy decisions that determine the overall direction of the revolutionary process and shape the organizational structures, mechanisms, and procedures for advancing that process.

In Cuba, such decisions would include, among other things, the mobilization of the population to produce 10 million tons of sugar in 1970, to institutionalize democratic centralist forms of organization in the 1970s, and to launch a major rectification campaign in 1986. Although it is clear that it occupies the commanding posts of both the party and the state in Cuba, I define the revolutionary leadership according to its decision-making function rather than its institutional location, as is more usual. Besides the well-known key figures like Fidel Castro and a few others, very little is known about who actually participates in making the most significant decisions in Cuba. Specifying only members of the Political Bureau or the Council of State would perhaps omit some important figures, while including all members of the Central Committee or the National Assembly would add in some unimportant ones. The point is that, in our current state of knowledge, we have no way of knowing where to draw the line; therefore, it seems prudent to use a functional, rather than a misleading institutional definition of the revolutionary leadership.

The terms "political cadres" and "old cadres" refer to the same group at different points of time, through 1970 and after 1970 respectively. The political cadres are those individuals who through 1970 entered intermediate-level occupations on the basis of their political reliability. The old cadres are those same individuals who after 1970 retained their intermediate-level positions without obtaining the secondary school degree that by then had officially become the minimum educational credential for these positions. After 1970, however, the old (political) cadres were gradually displaced by the new professionals, who began to enter these same occupations on the basis of educational credentials. Thus, the old (political) cadres and the new professionals are differentiated by their educational levels, not by their occupational positions.

I use the term "intermediate-level occupations" in both the prerevolutionary and postrevolutionary periods. For the first period, the term refers to the occupations of small business proprietor, manager, technician, professional, as given in the Cuban census of 1953. For the period after 1959, it refers to those occupations in the state, political, and mass organizations (i.e., excluding the relatively small and, until recently, diminishing private sector) that are not typically involved in making fundamental policy decisions, nor directly or predominantly take part in material or nonmaterial production processes, but rather design, organize, or direct these processes, and oversee and coordinate the activities of other individuals in these processes.

The first and second parts of this definition distinguish those employed in these occupations from revolutionary leaders and from workers, respectively. It should be clear from the third part of this definition that what is referred to is a very broad stratum of occupations. The lower level of this stratum consists in material production of what the Cubans call medium-level technicians (*técnicos medios*), who direct and control technical processes and coordinate the activities of other workers. In the hierarchy of Cuban labor categories, these stand just above skilled workers (*obreros calificados*), who do not engage in overseeing the work of others.[8] The lower level of the intermediate stratum in nonmaterial production includes individuals, such as primary or secondary schoolteachers, who design, direct, and oversee the processes of those under their supervision, such as their students' learning. The higher level of the whole stratum includes individuals who perform managerial, scientific, or technical work at the top level of the Communist Party or the state, teach in a university, or do research, depending on their expertise. Of course, between these higher and lower levels fall a wide variety of other occupational slots.

It should be noted that, although the content and context commonly makes clear which is meant, current Cuban terminology obscures the distinction drawn here between old (political) cadres and new professionals in intermediate-level occupations. Cubans sometimes refer to "new professionals," but with no regularity. They as easily speak of specialists, managers, or technicians trained by the revolution. They indiscriminately call all administrative personnel "cadres," and appear to have no special term for the old (political) cadres identified here. The fact that Cuban usage hides the distinction between old (political) cadres and new professionals, of course, heightens the significance of its disclosure here.

Sources of Evidence

I gained much of my sense of the actors and relationships that make up the Cuban stratification system through interviews in Cuba. But because of their necessarily informal character and nonscientific sampling, they could not serve as the primary empirical underpinning for the major themes and conclusions of this work. Cuba scholars have long been aware of the virtual impossibility of outsiders conducting scientific social research in Cuba. The few who have bravely tried have come away with suggestive impressions, but admittedly less than scientific results.[9] To avoid such an outcome, I have used the interviews I conducted very selectively, mostly to add color to parts of the argument and to corroborate information gathered from other sources.

For the most part, therefore, I have relied in this work on published sources, both primary and secondary. This is not a compilation of others' writings, however. This book breaks new ground: not only does it provide a variety of new quantitative estimates and time series, but it also explores a largely ignored topic and presents an unprecedented argument.

Relying so heavily on published sources, of course, has definite advantages. Such sources provide testimony from only a select group of witnesses, chosen not by the researcher but by those who control the printed media, but they are free of the bias that results from interaction between researcher and witness. A researcher may be led astray by such sources, but not because of any direct interaction with the witness.

Perhaps most important, published sources can be checked by other scholars. Any source has the disadvantages and advantages of its type. This simply underscores the need for all sources to be used carefully and critically, as I have attempted to do throughout this book. Since most of the sources are published, anyone who is interested can evaluate my success in this regard.

An Overview of the Book

This is a study of the relationship in revolutionary Cuba between social stratification and politics broadly conceived. Its major innovation is to widen the focus of analytic attention to identify and examine the salient actors at the intermediate level of Cuban society. In addition, it seeks to uncover typical patterns of conflict and cooperation between different types of intermediate-level actors and both the workers below them and the revolutionary leadership above them in decision-making power. Chapter 2 examines the inadequacies of the pre-revolutionary educational system, the exodus of U.S. nationals and some intermediate-level Cubans, and the policies of the revolutionary leadership. It considers the relative contribution of each to the scarcity, misallocation, and lack of skills that severely plagued the revolution in its early years.

Chapter 3 looks at the early educational and organizational responses of the revolutionary leadership to this skill problem. It argues that these responses were important in engendering the political-economic crisis of 1970, which led to a variety of changes that, among other things, gave rise to the new professionals.

Chapter 4 discusses the post-1970 structural and strategic reassessments that created the supply of new professionals through educational changes. This process of rectification brought on new democratic centralist political and economic structures, fostering the demand for new professions.

Chapter 5 examines various aspects of the decline of the old (political) cadres and the rise of the new professionals. It focuses on the revolutionary leadership's attempt to manage this transition after 1970 and on the makeup and formation of the new professionals.

Chapter 6 considers the problem of bureaucratic centralism

and underscores typical patterns of conflict and cooperation between old cadres, new professionals, revolutionary leaders, and workers in the Cuban economy from the mid-1970s to 1986.

Chapter 7 looks at the rectification campaign that the revolutionary leadership launched in 1986.

Chapter 8 concludes by examining the crisis that the revolution entered after 1989. This discussion will demonstrate the importance of the new professionals to the possible economic resolution and to the political dynamic of this crisis. This study will demonstrate that to understand Cuba today requires paying attention to the new professionals.

Notes

1. Figures from Andrew Zimbalist, "Dateline Cuba: Hanging on in Havana," *Foreign Policy* 90 (Spring 1993): 151-167.
2. By far the best discussion of Mas Canosa is by Gaeton Fonzi, "Who is Jorge Mas Canosa?," *Esquire*, January 1993, pp. 86-89, 119-22; useful information is also presented by George Gedda, "The Cuba Lobby," *Foreign Service Journal*, June 1993, pp. 24-29; and Peter Stone, "Cuba Clout," *National Journal*, 20 February 1993, pp. 449-53.
3. For evidence of these private rationales, see Morris H. Morley, *Imperial State and Revolution: The United States and Cuba, 1952-1986* (London: Cambridge University Press, 1987), pp. 191-92, 195.
4. See *Latin America Weekly Review*, 23 July 1992, p. 10.
5. In recent years, Cuba scholars have mentioned Cuba's new professionals with increasing frequency. Still, the only extended examinations of the new professionals that have preceded this one are: Frank T. Fitzgerald, *Managing Socialism: From Old Cadres to New Professionals in Revolutionary Cuba* (New York: Praeger, 1990); and Thomas C. Dalton, *"Everything Within the Revolution": Cuban Strategies for Social Development Since 1960* (Boulder, CO: Westview Press, 1993).
6. H. Gordon Skilling, "The Party, Opposition, and Interest Groups

in Communist Politics," in Kurt London (ed.), *The Soviet Union: A Half-Century of Communism* (Baltimore: Johns Hopkins Press, 1968), p. 122.

7. Eliot Friedson, "The Theory of Professions: State of the Art," in Robert Dingwall and Philip Lewis (eds.), *The Sociology of the Professions* (London: Macmillan, 1983), p. 23.

8. Officially, medium-level technicians and all occupational categories above them in the Cuban system of labor categories require at least a secondary school degree. Skilled workers, on the other hand, are officially required to have only a diploma from a polytechnical school, which requires fewer years of schooling. See UNCTAD, *Health and Education Technology in Cuba* (New York: United Nations Organization, 1979), p. 28. The education of Cuban medium-level technicians and skilled workers differs not only in length but also in content. The Ministry of Education once described the classroom time of medium-level technicians as "30 percent practical" and of skilled workers as "60 percent practical." See Ministerio de Educación, *Cuba: organización de la educación, 1981-1983, informe a la XXXIX Conferencia Internacional de Educación, Genebra, Suiza* (Havana: 1984), p. 213.

9. This is particularly true of Marifeli Pérez-Stable, *Politics and Conciencia in Revolutionary Cuba, 1959-1984* (Ph.D. diss., State University of New York at Stony Brook, 1985), which both illustrates and discusses in some detail the problems confronted by outsiders in doing social research in Cuba; also see the excellent discussion of Linda Fuller, "Fieldwork in Forbidden Terrain: The U.S. State and the Case of Cuba," *The American Sociologist* 19, no. 2 (Summer 1988): 99-120.

Chapter 2
The Young Revolution Confronts a Skill Shortage

After a military coup brought Fulgencio Batista to power in 1952, a diversity of individuals and organizations allied against his dictatorial and widely hated regime. Once the anti-Batista forces triumphed in early 1959, however, their always uneasy alliance quickly fractured. The old regime's opponents immediately vied with one another for control of the new regime and for the right to determine the future shape of Cuban society.

As this struggle progressed, the forces headed by Fidel Castro consolidated their political control and undertook a massive redistribution of income and wealth. Between 1959 and 1963, the Castro government halved rents, increased wages and employment, expanded health and education services, and put 70 percent of the land and 90 to 100 percent of industry, commerce, banking, and foreign trade in the hands of the state.[1]

Wage workers and peasants rallied to the new regime as it advanced from reform to socialist revolution, while the country's large property owners rapidly moved into a counterrevolutionary alliance with the United States. Situated between these two poles, Cuba's intermediate strata—professionals, managers, intelligentsia, and skilled workforce—split into revolutionary and counterrevolutionary factions.

As a viable political alternative, the U.S.-supported counterrevolution was relatively short-lived, and was decisively defeated, along with the U.S.-sponsored armed invasion, at the

Bay of Pigs in April 1961. Even after that, however, the United States continued its offensive against the revolution, an offensive that hit all Cubans but targeted, first and foremost, the country's intermediate strata. The United States, for example, continued to embargo and blockade the Cuban economy, knowing that intermediate-level Cubans stood to lose palpably from their country's economic isolation.

The United States also continued to encourage Cubans, especially from the intermediate strata, to flee the island as political refugees. By squeezing intermediate-level Cubans at home and enticing them abroad, the United States hoped to rob the revolution of important skilled personnel. In the revolution's early years, in fact, many intermediate-level Cubans fled the island, taking their skills with them. This exodus contributed significantly to the skill problem that plagued the revolution even beyond its first decade.

The Revolution's Educational Inheritance

The skill problem, however, predated the revolution's early struggles and was aggravated but not caused by Cuba's postrevolutionary exodus. Cuba's problem of scarce, misallocated, or altogether missing skills resulted directly from the inadequate educational system of its colonial and neocolonial past. Understanding Cuba's skill problem requires, before looking at the postrevolutionary exodus, first examining the prerevolutionary legacy in education.

Cuba's skill problem manifested itself at all occupational levels. At the lower levels, it took the form of widespread illiteracy and ignorance. According to the official census of 1953, of the 4.4 million Cubans over the age of nine, 23.6 percent were illiterate, a figure that rose to 41.7 percent in the countryside.[2] In May 1963, Cuban investigators found that, of the more than one million workers who they tested, 55 percent could demonstrate knowledge equal to only that taught in the first two grades of school; 28.1 percent, only to that taught in grades three though six; and only 5.5 percent equal to that taught in the first year of secondary school.[3]

At occupational levels above this, the skill problem showed up in personnel who often were not even minimally prepared for their jobs. The chief executive at the revolution's new Foreign Trade Bank (*Banco Para el Comercio Exterior*), for example, was a twenty-seven-year-old rebel army major with only some premedical training at the university. His deputy had studied to be an economist, but had experience only in journalism. Apart from one doctor who helped import pharmaceuticals, the bank totally lacked technicians familiar with Cuba's requirements for replacement parts and raw materials. A young man with six months' experience at the National Bank was put in charge of the country's imports; a twenty-three-year-old, who had worked in an export house for a few years, was made responsible for several hundred million dollars worth of exports.[4]

The picture was similar in other areas too. A 1964 study of 2,000 state farms found that 40 percent of their administrators had less than four years of schooling.[5] Six years later, the average educational level of all of the country's administrative personnel still did not exceed the sixth grade. As Fidel Castro remarked in 1970: "Signs of illiteracy and semiliteracy can be found in many men in positions of responsibility."[6]

Yet it has been said that at the time of the revolutionary triumph, Cuba possessed the most advanced educational system in Latin America.[7] Such a comparison, however, said less about the level of Cuban education at the time than it did about the general backwardness of Latin American education. The proper benchmark for evaluating education in prerevolutionary Cuba was not education in other Latin American countries, but the promise of educational opportunity that had been held out to the Cuban people, even embodied in Cuban law, since the turn of the century.

The Cuban Constitution of 1901 promised no less than free compulsory schooling for all primary-school-age children, that is, for all six- to fourteen-year-olds. Various laws and decrees throughout the first half of the century—in 1909, 1922, 1940, and again in 1946—reaffirmed this promise. And, in fact, enrollment at the primary level rose to 46 percent of the relevant age group by 1909, and to 63 percent by 1926.[8] But over the next three decades, this momentum was lost. The proportion of primary-school-age children actually attending school, according to the 1953 census, had dropped to 55.6 percent. In the countryside, only 38.7 percent of children at this age were enrolled; and, in the poor, sugar-growing province of Oriente, only 26.9 percent.[9]

With attendance so low at the "compulsory" primary level, it is not surprising that it was even lower at the secondary level, for the fifteen- to nineteen-year-olds who were not required by Cuban law to attend school. Just 16.4 percent of this age category were still in school in 1953, and only 11 percent in the poor, rural province of Pinar del Río.[10] It is also not surprising that, of college-age youths in the twenty- to twenty-four-year-old group, only 18 percent were still in school, and in the rural areas, merely 6.5 percent.[11]

The deficiencies of the prerevolutionary educational system also showed up in the few number of grades completed by the Cuban population. According to the 1953 census, more than 1.5 million Cubans, or 31 percent of those over five years of age, had not even completed the first grade, and many of these had never attended school at all. Only 56.5 percent of those over fourteen years of age, moreover, had finished from five to eight grades; only 5.6 percent of those over nineteen, any secondary grade; only 2.0 percent of those over twenty-four, some level of university education.[12]

But even when Cuban youths had attended school and completed certain grades, their skill levels were still often low. Although no achievement data exist for Cuban students in this period, the low quality of their education was indicated in a variety of ways.

First, even though the amount of resources devoted to education in prerevolutionary Cuba's educational resources was respectable by international standards—it stood at an estimated 23 percent of the state budget and at about 3 percent of national income in 1955 and 1956[13]—maladministration and corruption ate up much of this. As one Cuban scholar commented, prior to the revolution a "certain Minister of Education was known by his practice of selling classrooms, another by the use of ministerial funds for campaigning purposes, and another by the physical appropriation of cash for himself from the treasury vaults."[14] Nor was corruption limited to the ministerial level. Tenured teachers frequently collected salaries without teaching at all: they simply hired untrained stand-ins at low pay, pocketed the difference in pesos, and never showed up for class.[15]

Second, education in prerevolutionary Cuba used outmoded methods and materials. As a later United Nations study would point out, curricula, teaching methods, textbooks, and other course materials were short on scientific content and excessively verbalistic, abstract, and formal. Rather than attempting to develop inquisitive minds and a scientific-experimental attitude, prerevolutionary Cuban education encouraged students to memorize and recite the words of teachers and texts.[16]

Third, the content of education in prerevolutionary Cuba was ill-suited to the country's social and economic needs.

Although Cuba was, and is, primarily an agricultural country, in the 1955 to 1956 academic year only 3.7 percent of its university students were majoring in agricultural sciences, while some 23.0 percent were studying humanities.[17] At the secondary level, the country possessed six agricultural schools, but with a capacity of only thirty students each.[18] In 1953, as a consequence, Cuba had only 294 agronomists and 355 veterinarians out of a labor force of almost two million workers.[19]

In short, Cuba's prerevolutionary educational system taught too few students, poorly taught those it did teach, and taught them the wrong things. It left the most downtrodden sectors of the Cuban population hobbled by illiteracy, the wider society suffering from misallocated, scarce, or altogether lacking skills, and the new revolutionary regime confronting a serious skill problem. Given this inheritance, it is no wonder that, as will be seen in Chapter 3, the revolutionary leadership immediately attempted to expand and transform the country's educational system.

The Early Exodus from Revolutionary Cuba

As already mentioned, Cuba's inadequate pool of skills was depleted further in the early years of the revolution, when many skilled individuals fled the country. Wealthy Cubans, unable to maintain their class privileges under the new revolutionary regime, were among the first to leave. They were soon joined by U.S. citizens who had been employed in Cuba and by Cubans from the intermediate level of society. These latter two groups each left for reasons of their own, but also because they were encouraged to leave by the United States, as part of its anti-Castro strategy.

Many U.S. citizens in Cuba had possessed managerial and technical skills, and had occupied important posts in the U.S.

corporations that controlled much of the prerevolutionary economy. Although lack of data makes estimating their number impossible, most of the higher administrative and technical personnel working for U.S. concerns in Cuba had been U.S. nationals. In the U.S. oil refineries, for example, while Cubans took care of maintenance and cleaning, operated cars and trucks, and served as mechanics, U.S. personnel commonly directed operations.[20]

Such highly skilled U.S. nationals did not leave Cuba simply because businesses were being taken over by the new revolutionary regime as it was nationalizing the economy. They were encouraged to leave by the U.S. government, as the oil conflict of the early years of the revolution demonstrates.[21]

Controlling the island's only oil refineries and about 15 percent of all of its total direct foreign investments, U.S. petroleum companies occupied an important place in the Cuban economy. The revolutionary government, consequently, announced a new petroleum law in November 1959 to extend state control over these companies. This law stipulated that unexploited concessions would revert to the Cuban state and that royalties paid by U.S. oil companies would go up some 10 to 60 percent.

A few months later, in February 1960, the Cuban government struck a deal with the Soviet Union to have the latter supply from 30 to 50 percent of Cuba's annual crude oil needs. This agreement greatly benefited the Cubans by allowing them to barter sugar for oil rather than pay in scarce hard currency, and by providing them with a better price than U.S. companies offered. Although the U.S. companies at first appeared resigned to operating according to the new rules of the game, the U.S. government encouraged them to resist, and organized and coordinated their actions as part of a general counterrevolutionary strategy. Eventually, with State Department encouragement and support, U.S. companies refused to refine Soviet crude oil; they were then nationalized by the revolutionary government.

Along the way, however, the U.S. government and corporate sector working in alliance attempted to influence the policies of the revolutionary regime by squeezing the Cuban economy. On May 11, 1960, for example, after the Soviet-Cuban oil agreement had been announced but before U.S. companies were asked to refine the Soviet oil, Texaco officials met with Assistant Secretary of State for Inter-American Affairs Roy Rubottom to find out how the company should respond when asked to refine the Soviet oil. According to the State Department record of the conversation:

> Mr. Rubottom said that at no time had he or Mr. [Treasury Secretary C. Douglas] Dillon or other high officials of the Department suggested that the companies should continue to ship crude into Cuba if such action was not in accord with their own overall commercial judgment. ... He observed that the economic noose seems to be tightening around Castro's neck and the country shows signs of economic strains; that it has always been the Department's thought that the best possible solution for the Cuban situation would be a Cuban solution. At the same time it is our thought that at some stage we might be able and wish to contribute to this solution. This sort of pressure which the petroleum companies can exert is one of the pressures which the Department has always had in mind.[22]

With this implicit State Department directive in hand, Texaco and the other U.S. oil companies immediately began to slow their Cuban operations and to repatriate their highly skilled U.S. personnel. By the end of May, for example, Texaco had withdrawn twenty-six of its thirty-two U.S. employees. Even though these and other withdrawn U.S. citizens did not add up to large numbers of personnel, because of the critical posts they had occupied in the Cuban economy, they were never-theless an important element in the early flight of skilled personnel from the island—their exodus aggravated the revolution's already-massive skill problem.

The numerically larger exodus of Cuban nationals, of course, worsened the country's skill problem even more. Nevertheless, although Cuba's postrevolutionary refugees have been studied much over the years, no one else has ever attempted to utilize what is known about the refugee popula-tion and the labor force it left behind to gain a measure of the quantitative impact of the exodus on the skill level of the remaining Cuban population.

Much is known about who left but little about who stayed, even though it is relatively easy to estimate the relevant charac-teristics of the remaining population by simple subtraction.

Practically all large property owners left the island shortly after the revolution. They were joined by many others, espe-cially from the intermediate strata. These professionals, tech-nicians, managers, and small business proprietors, with their families, were overrepresented in the early years of the exodus from Cuba (see Table 2.1 in appendix). Although those in intermediate-level occupations were estimated to be less than 10 percent of the Cuban labor force in 1959, they made up almost 40 percent of the refugees between 1959 and 1962 who had been in the Cuban labor force.

While an estimated 34,570 intermediate-level labor force participants, or 16.6 percent of those in Cuba in 1959, actually had left the country by the end of 1962, 83.4 percent—the vast majority—still remained. When traced through 1980, the num-ber of refugees from intermediate-level occupations added up to an estimated 69,858, or 33.5 percent of the total number of incumbents of those occupations in 1959 (see Table 2.2 in appendix). The loss of almost 17 percent of all intermediate-level personnel in the revolution's first few years, combined with the loss in the 1960s and 1970s of over one-third of the intermediate personnel with which it started, have been a continuous drag on efforts to develop the country's economy (even though this latter loss would be more than compensated by dramatic educational growth, as described in Chapter 5).

The question arises, nonetheless: Why had so many inter-mediate-level job holders stayed in Cuba? Certainly, a range of factors had their effect: revolutionary commitment; national, community, and family ties; simple inertia. But as mentioned above, the United States pulled in the opposite direction to uproot Cubans, especially intermediate-level Cubans. The available information is insufficiently detailed to provide a defini-tive explanation.

A closer look at the occupational breakdown of the early intermediate-level refugees (see Table 2.1) suggests a possible answer. Those whose skills would prove most out of tune with the new revolutionary society were more likely to leave and were fewer in number; those whose skills would retain more of their usefulness were more likely to stay in the country and were greater in number.

The smallest category of intermediate-level occupations, after all, was the one most affected by the exodus, that of lawyers and judges. These occupations, tightly wedded to the old legal system, were capable of adapting only with great difficulty to new forms of popular justice, like the People's Courts. One would expect legal professionals to exhibit, in Thorstein Veblen's terms, a "trained incapacity" to integrate themselves into, or even to accept, the revolutionary process.

One might also expect the same of many in the middle-size category of intermediate-level occupations: professionals and semi-professionals. The single biggest group in this category was school and university teachers. Although many of these supported the revolutionary movement, about half of them joined the early exodus,[23] making up a large percentage of the refugees in the professional and semi-professional category. Many teachers might exhibit a trained incapacity to adapt to the revolutionary process and to accept the new revolutionary ideology by virtue of their intellectual formation in pre-revolutionary schools and their role as conveyors to the younger generation of conventional culture. Acceptance of the new ideology, after all, would have brought into question much that teachers had been taught to teach and much that they had taught.

Many Cuban teachers, in fact, viewed revolutionary changes in the curriculum as pro-revolutionary distortions of truth. As two exiled former teachers explained their views of the early revolutionary process in the schools:

> We were supposed to eliminate all the materials that were not revolutionary in nature. For instance, the history books were completely eliminated. We were given guidelines about how to explain the different events in Cuban history. We were not supposed to take on our own or any explanations that had not already been confirmed by militia men that were there two or three times a week more or less instructing and telling the principal and teachers what to do and say. ...
>
> There were new books; in general most of them had political emphasis in the texts.[24]

What was taught before supposedly was pure, apolitical truth. The new changes, therefore, represented for these teachers gross political distortions.

Such teachers, moreover, did not teach just subject matter. They also tried to mold students to the authority relations of the school, which typically mirrored the wider relations of society. Any attempt by the revolutionary forces to alter authority in the schools, therefore, was likely to be perceived by many teachers as illegitimate. Consider these quotes from two exiled Cuban former teachers:

> Students did not behave with the same discipline that they had before. Some of them felt very powerful, either because their families were strong supporters of the government or because they themselves had won some reputation as revolutionaries. Of course, they had a new weapon to intimidate everybody in the school, even classmates; that was to accuse them of being counterrevolutionaries.

> Most [students] were our enemies and were spies. They watched the teachers all the time and the way we behaved about the revolution. In each classroom the principal had some students whose job was to watch the teachers.[25]

This may help to explain why legal and educational professionals—the smallest and the middle-sized categories of intermediate-level occupations—showed a relatively higher propensity to join the exodus from Cuba. But why did so few managers and executives—the largest category of intermediate-level occupations—leave?

Part of the answer may be that this category contained some (the census data are insufficiently broken down to tell how many) small business proprietors.[26] Although many of these no doubt left Cuba in reaction to the early measures of the revolutionary regime, many stayed and did quite well through much of the 1960s.

According to one account, the new regime's difficulties with planning and economic controls allowed certain private enterprises to develop more or less spontaneously and to dominate the commercial trade network, especially in food. Of the commercial trade enterprises operating in 1967, in fact, 73.6 percent belonged to the private sector. Most of these businesses were very small, but a few were larger: three private enterprises, for example, reportedly each did more than 500,000 pesos' worth of business with state enterprises in the first half of 1967.

The government did not move against the small business sector until the Revolutionary Offensive of 1968, when it nationalized 58,012 private concerns. Thus, many small proprietors probably stayed in Cuba because until 1968 they could do quite well.[27]

Second, managers and executives found many of their economically relevant skills in even greater demand and their chances for acquiring higher positions greatly improved. As Donald Bray and Timothy Harding observed in the mid-1970s:

> Although there were many working-class people in high positions, most of the high government posts and the majority of the middle-level bureaucracy ... were manned by middle-class individuals who had not been Communists but were nevertheless dedicated to the Revolution. ... Most middle-class administrators, technicians, guides and translators hold more responsible positions today than they would have held before the Revolution. This shift has occurred because foreigners no longer make the fundamental decisions affecting Cuba, and also, because of the emigration of skilled people and the explosion of new services and production, anyone with skill in Cuba rises rapidly to top positions.[28]

Many managers and executives, in other words, directly benefited from the nationalization of U.S. property, from the exodus of other skilled Cubans, and from the revolutionary transformation of the economy.

If many of the revolution's intermediate-level posts were filled by members of the country's prerevolutionary intermediate strata, this does not mean that most of the intermediate actors who stayed in Cuba were absorbed into these posts. There is no way of knowing, in fact, what proportion rose to higher positions, what proportion stayed at about the same level, and what proportion moved down, even to manual tasks. That many were in this latter category in the 1960s, however, is indicated by the subsequent statements of revolutionary leaders. These criticized the earlier tendency to discriminate against prerevolutionary incumbents of intermediate-level posts, because such discrimination further depleted the revolution's available pool of skills.

Carlos Rafael Rodríguez, for one, suggested in 1972 that revolutionary leaders had not always recognized that the prerevolutionary intermediate strata fell into three distinct categories: (1) those with a socialist and nationalist consciousness, who were quickly integrated into the revolutionary process; (2) those with a capitalist and North American consciousness, who rapidly left the island in the first few years; and (3) those with a nonsocialist, even capitalist, consciousness, whose national consciousness nevertheless remained intact. According to Rodríguez, the revolution could have integrated many in this latter category; but, instead, the revolution lost skills by discriminating against them.[29]

Although many who suffered such discrimination probably joined the exodus, others endured in Cuba. I interviewed a man in 1980 who before the revolution had been a college-educated technician for one of the U.S. oil companies in Cuba.[30] In the 1960s, authorities prevented him from pursuing this or any other technical occupation, and forced him into various types of manual labor, usually in the sugar sector. Other than protesting to me that he never had opposed the revolution, I have no way of knowing the character of his political consciousness or activities in the early years of the revolution. But when I spoke with him much later, he expressed great pride in the revolution's accomplishments. He was also proud to again be a technician in the now-Cuban oil industry and to have three children working in or training for professional occupations; his oldest child was a university professor and his two younger children were both university students.

In his own terms, this individual's endurance obviously had paid off. The stories of many other intermediate-level Cubans who had been discriminated against in the 1960s presumably turned out less happily.

In summary, the Cuban revolution began with few skills for reasons both political and educational. Cuba's problem of scarce, misallocated, or nonexistent skills arose directly from the inadequacies of its prerevolutionary educational system, and was aggravated considerably by the early revolutionary struggles. Even though the vast majority of intermediate-level Cubans remained on the island, enough left to seriously harm the country's already poor skill profile. Among those who stayed in Cuba, moreover, some suffered official discrimination, which further depleted the revolution's pool of skills. The severity of the revolution's skill problem called forth a variety of official responses throughout the 1960s.

Notes

1. José Acosta, "Cuba: de la neocolonia a la construcción del socialismo (II)," *Economía y Desarrollo* 19 (November/December 1973): 79.
2. Oficina Nacional de los Censos Demográfica y Electora, *Censos de población, viviendos y electoral* (Havana: 1953), p. xxxix.
3. UNCTAD, *Health and Education Technology in Cuba* (New York: United Nations Organization, 1979), p. 11.
4. Edward Boorstein, *The Economic Transformation of Cuba* (New York: Monthly Review Press, 1968), pp. 63–64.
5. Cited in Nelson P. Valdés, *Cuba: socialismo democrático o bureaucratismo colectivista* (Bogotá: Ediciones Tercer Mundo,. 1973), p. 19.
6. Fidel Castro, "Report on the Cuban Economy" in Rolando

Bonachea and Nelson Valdés (eds.), *Cuba in Revolution* (Garden City, NY: Doubleday, 1972), p. 338.
7. CEPAL, *Cuba: estilo de desarrollo y políticos sociales* (Cerro del Agua, Mexico: Siglo Veintiuno Editores, 1980), p. 87.
8. UNCTAD, p. 3.
9. *Censos de población*, p. xxxviii.
10. Ibid., p. xxxix.
11. Author's computations based on ibid., p. 99.
12. Author's computations based on ibid., p. 119.
13. UNCTAD, p. 4.
14. Jorge García Gallo, "Bosquejo general del desarrollo de la educación en Cuba (Tercera Parte)," *Educación*, July/September 1974, p. 32.
15. UNCTAD, p. 4.
16. Ibid.
17. Ibid., p. 32.
18. Ibid., p. 27.
19. *Censos de población*, p. 204.
20. Boorstein, *Economic Transformation of Cuba*, p. 55.
21. The following account of the oil conflict is taken from the excellent discussion by Morris Morley, *Toward a Theory of Imperial Politics: United States Policy and the Processes of State Formation, Disintegration and Consolidation in Cuba, 1898–1978* (Ph.D. diss., State University of New York at Binghamton, 1980), pp. 428–38.
22. Memorandum of Conversation, U.S. Department of State, May 11, 1960, Subject: "Difficulties of the Texas Company in Cuba with regard to dollar remittances and concern at possibility it will be asked to refine Russian crude oil," 837.131/5-1160 (declassified Freedom of Information Act), cited in ibid., p. 430.
23. Author's interview HG01.80, with a Cuban government official.
24. Eugene F. Provenzano and Concepción García, "Exiled Teachers and the Cuban Revolution," *Cuban Studies/Estudios Cubanos* 13, no. 1 (Winter 1983): 2, 7.
25. Ibid., p. 9.
26. See *Censos de población*, p. 204.
27. All data on small proprietors from Hector Ayala Castro,

"Transformación de propiedad en el período 1964-1980," *Economía y Desarrollo* 68 (May/June 1982): 11-25.

28. Donald W. Bray and Timothy F. Harding, "Cuba," in Ronald H. Chilcote and Joel C. Edelstein (eds.), *Latin America: The Struggle with Dependency and Beyond* (Cambridge, Massachusetts: Schenkman Publishing, 1974), pp. 620-21.

29. Carlos Rafael Rodríguez, "En el proceso de construcción del socialismo la política debe tener prioridad," *Economía y Desarrollo* 14 (November/December 1972): 144-57.

30. Author's interview HNGT4.80.

Chapter 3
The 1960s:
Development Strategies, Experiments, and Crisis

As Cuba's revolutionary leadership took control of most productive property and consolidated its political base by redistributing income, it also attended to economic development. In its first development strategy (1961 to 1963), the regime strove to move away from sugar monoculture through immediate agricultural diversification and industrialization.[1] But this strategy was both poorly suited to Cuba's resource and skill endowments at the time and severely impeded by the U.S. economic embargo and blockade.[2] Balance of trade and other economic difficulties soon emerged, and the revolution had to pursue a new strategy.

In its second development strategy (1964 to 1970), the regime reverted to agricultural specialization and undertook a big push to produce a record 10 million tons of sugar in 1970.[3] In 1964, the Soviet Union facilitated and helped insulate this strategy from U.S. economic aggression by guaranteeing a reliable and expanding market for Cuban sugar: The Soviets agreed to increase their imports of sugar from Cuba to 5 million tons annually from 1968 through 1970 and to pay the then-high price of 6.11 cents per pound. The Cubans would sell the other five tons of sugar on the world market for hard currency. Export of this 10 million tons of sugar, it was hoped, would allow Cuba to begin equalizing its balance of payments and start importing sufficient capital goods for a new, more secure round of industrialization. Emphasizing sugar and other agricultural products, this second development strategy better suited Cuba's conditions of soil and climate and its accumulated know-how and skills.

Still, as the revolutionary government pursued its second strategy, it went beyond just accepting Cuba's endowment of skills—it confronted the skill problem from two sides. On the supply side, even before it instituted the first development strategy, the revolutionary leadership pushed to increase the supply of skills by expanding and transforming education. On the demand side, especially during the second development strategy, the revolutionary leadership tried to minimize the demand for relatively skilled intermediate-level personnel: It introduced unorthodox organizational and motivational mechanisms designed to limit the need for skills. It also increasingly used political, rather than vocational or educational, criteria to fill administrative posts, and thus gave rise to a sizeable group of political cadres acting as administrators.

Although the second development strategy increased Cuba's economic ties to the Soviet bloc, Cuban leaders charted an independent policy course in this period, sometimes defiantly. Internationally, they spurned the moderate coalition politics of Soviet-allied Communist Parties and promoted armed struggle, especially in Latin America. Domestically, they veered from Soviet notions of how to construct socialism and embarked on their own *fidelista* path, rejecting reliance on material incentives for workers to spur productivity.

Most economists have criticized the second development strategy and its ten-million-ton sugar harvest goal as overly ambitious; others defended it on strictly economic grounds.[4] But beyond arguments and intentions, in practice the combination of the second development strategy with the Cubans' *fidelista* organizational and motivational mechanisms proved volatile. This mix would explode in the political and economic crisis of 1970.

Increasing the Skill Supply

The revolutionary government began expanding education almost immediately after coming to power. The most dramatic push, however, came in 1961, proclaimed the "Year of Education," with its widely respected literacy campaign. This campaign, which lasted from January 1 to December 22, 1961, spread over the island with the slogans "The People Should Teach the People" and "If You Do Not Know, Learn; If You Know, Teach!" In all, an estimated 271,000 Cubans participated in this campaign as voluntary teachers. In only one year, these volunteers reduced Cuba's illiteracy rate from 23.6 to 3.9 percent.[5]

The literacy campaign had other results as well. It helped, for example, to integrate town and country and to galvanize support for revolutionary goals by bringing urban and rural populations into direct contact. It also gave officials experience in mobilizing and organizing the population on a broad scale, and it allowed many youths who for one reason or another had not participated in the anti-Batista struggle to demonstrate and hone their leadership skills. Finally, Cuba's literacy campaign whetted the appetite of many Cubans to upgrade their cultural development, and thus prepared the way for further expansion of the educational system.[6]

Although the literacy campaign was an astounding success, it was merely a beginning. In order to maintain the higher literacy levels gained by thousands during the campaign, the new skills had to be built upon and reinforced. Within a month of the campaign's end, the revolutionary government addressed this need by forming a department of adult education within the Ministry of Education. Out of this eventually grew a full-scale adult education system parallel to the regular system at the primary and secondary levels.[7]

Enrollment in adult education rose dramatically from 66,577 students in the 1960 to 1961 school year to a peak of 842,024 students in 1964 to 1965, but then plummeted to 306,917 students in 1969 to 1970 (see Table 3.1 in appendix). As a result, the literacy campaign's "Battle for the Sixth Grade," which had been launched in 1964 to bring the adult population up to the sixth grade level, had not been won by the end of the 1960s. This drop was also a likely factor in the rise of the illiteracy rate to a reported 12.9 percent by 1970.[8]

The dramatic drop in adult education enrollments in the second half of the 1960s was a direct result of the second economic development strategy. Not only did the push to produce 10 million tons of sugar gobble up resources that could have been used to educate adults, it also drew many adults away from classrooms and into the sugar fields as voluntary laborers. Moreover, the trade unions and other mass organizations, the institutions largely responsible for furthering adult education during the second strategy, were seriously weakened.

Unlike adult education, primary-level schooling continued to expand throughout the first decade of the revolution. In the 1958 to 1959 school year, 625,729 students were enrolled at the primary level; by 1969 to 1970 this figure had climbed to 1,427,607 (see Table 3.1).

This steady increase, however, hid a complex of problems. Many students who had either dropped out of school during the year or failed had to repeat their grade. Of the class that entered first grade in 1964 and was scheduled to complete sixth grade in 1970, only 20.7 percent were actually graduated on time.[9] Much of the expansion of primary education was made necessary, in other words, by the inefficiency of the system itself.

Secondary-level education in Cuba also expanded dramatically with the revolution. However, by 1970 to 1971 only 63.8 percent of thirteen- to sixteen-year-old Cubans were in school. Although this was a vast improvement over the 1953 figure of 39.8 percent, by the end of the 1960s Cuban secondary education still required further expansion.[10] Moreover, as in adult education, secondary education enrollments began to contract in the late 1960s (see Table 3.1). Enrollments at this level steadily increased from 88,135 students in 1958 to 1959 to 288,748 students by 1967 to 1968, and then dipped slightly to 276,209 students by 1969 to 1970.

This decline can be attributed in part to the stagnation of the number of primary school graduates, which meant fewer students ready to begin secondary training. As well, many secondary education students were probably pulled out of the classroom and into the sugar fields during the second development strategy.

Through the 1960s, higher education, although considerably transformed, was the least expansive level within the education system as a whole. At the time of the revolutionary triumph, Cuba possessed only three public universities, at Havana, Las Villas, and Santiago, one private university, and several private colleges. During the late 1950s, the embattled Batista had closed the public institutions because of the opposition they spawned. In turn, he allowed the private institutions, with their more supportive or quiescent faculty and students, to remain open. Soon after the triumph, the revolutionary leadership reopened the public universities, and in 1961 it abolished the private ones.

In 1962, the new leadership consolidated all institutions of higher education under the Ministry of Education, and promulgated a far-reaching reform of the whole higher education system.[11] But expansion of higher education did not immediately follow. As late as 1974 to 1975, in fact, the country still had only five higher education centers.[12]

Higher education enrollments actually dropped in the early years of the revolution to reach a low of 17,257 in 1962 to 1963, and they did not recover their 1959 to 1960 level until 1964 to 1965 (see Table 3.1). Scarcity of qualified secondary school graduates in this period probably accounted for part of this drop. But perhaps more significantly, higher education enrollments dropped due to the intense ideological struggle that took place in the universities over the extension of higher education to workers and peasants and over the character and content of the education that should be provided. Although the majority of the student body supported the new government's push to revolutionize higher education, many faculty and some students did not. These opponents often left the university to join counterrevolutionary organizations or to join the exodus out of Cuba.[13]

After this initial drop, higher education enrollments began a steady, if relatively gradual, climb to 35,137 in 1969 to 1970. However, much of this expansion was wasted. In 1968 to 1969, for example, a full 50 percent of first-year university students failed to pass in their initial year. Cuban researchers did not begin systematic study of the predominant causes of failure until 1969 to 1970. And higher education authorities did not introduce corrective measures until 1971 to 1972.[14]

The pattern of higher education enrollments can be illustrated in another manner. As the educational level of the population rose over the 1960s, enrollments at the primary level decreased as a percentage of total enrollments, while enrollments at the secondary level increased (see Table 3.2 in appendix). This increase, however, did not extend to the higher education level. As a percentage of total enrollments, higher education enrollments dropped from 2.4 percent in 1959 to 1960 to 1.8 percent in 1970 to 1971.

There are two additional explanations for the relatively slow growth and relative decline of higher education enrollments as a percentage of total enrollments in the 1960s. First and most obvious is that before higher education could expand dramatically both primary and secondary education had to expand and become more efficient; the latter two levels received the most attention in the 1960s. Second, due to the scarcity of skilled personnel in the 1960s, many would-be candidates for university training were pulled into jobs rather than into classrooms. One can find in Cuba many personnel in intermediate occupations who gained undergraduate or graduate degrees relatively late because their education was interrupted in the 1960s by the needs of economic development.[15]

The 1960s saw higher education in Cuba transformed in character and content. The 1962 reform of higher education eliminated tenure for faculty members, set faculty salaries, restructured the university governance system, set entrance requirements for students, and much else. But perhaps the most significant change was the restructuring of course and subject areas and the redistribution of enrollment by subject area. As the reform document emphasized, Cuban education suffered from a lack of fit between the nature of the knowledge imparted and the needs of economic development. This the reform sought to change.[16]

Enrollment in higher education subject areas changed considerably in the 1960s (see Table 3.3 in appendix). On the one hand, subject areas directly related to economic development or social service needs expanded the most rapidly. Between 1959 and 1970, agricultural sciences enrollments went from 759 to 5,154, an increase of 579.1 percent. That this was the most expansive subject area reflected the agricultural emphasis of the second development strategy and the 10-million-ton sugar goal. In this same period, the subject areas of technology, natural and exact sciences, and medical sciences experienced substantial but more moderate enrollment increases. In contrast, subject areas not directly related to economic development were deemphasized in the 1960s; enrollments in humanities, social sciences, and art actually fell 42 percent.

Less obviously consistent with the overall pattern, however, are the enrollment drops in education and economic studies.[17] Education enrollments dropped in the 1960s from 5,180 to 1,627, or by 68.6 percent. This might at first be surprising, because, as already seen, both primary and secondary enrollments—and therefore the need for teachers—increased in these years. Some of this drop in education enrollments can probably be explained by an excessive enthusiasm for the use of "amateur" teachers that resulted from the remarkable results obtained in the literacy campaign.[18] In fact, scarcity of resources made it imperative for the Cubans to rely for many years on less-trained teachers who were often only a few grades ahead of their pupils. But this could hardly explain an actual drop in education enrollments. As the Cubans eventually recognized, this drop was excessive and aggravated many of the problems in the educational system touched on above.[19] But this drop would not be reversed until after 1970.

The 76.4 percent drop of enrollments in economic studies between 1959 to 1960 and 1969 to 1970 is especially interesting, because it reflects the major policy shifts of the revolutionary leadership over the 1960s. This drop was probably not linear. In the early 1960s, before and during the first economic development strategy, the leadership greatly emphasized the need for increased numbers of economic professionals.[20] As early as March 2, 1960, then-Minister of Industry Ernesto "Che"

Guevara, in a speech at the University of Havana, called for establishing a school for training Cuban economic professionals to replace the many foreign ones on whom the revolution was dependent for teaching, and for planning and administering its increasingly collectivized economy. But due to the intense political struggle at the University of Havana in this period, no such school was established until the reform of higher education in 1962.

Even then, however, the need for trained economic planners, evaluators, and analysts was too great to wait the five years required to produce the first graduates. As a result, in the same year an emergency course for planners was implemented to train economic professionals in 1.5 (later two) years. By 1964, this emergency course was eliminated, perhaps because it was not doing the job, and its students were placed in the regular courses at the University of Havana. In this same period, various ministries set up their own crash courses to train their own economic personnel as quickly as possible.

Cuba's initial attempts to train economic professionals suffered from the country's lack of a strong tradition of economic studies. This weakness coupled with the early exodus of a majority of the members of the business faculty (*Facultad de Ciencias Comerciales*) at the University of Havana, resulted in a severe shortage of teachers. To address this problem, about forty revolutionary students were chosen for intense preparation by Latin American and Soviet professors to become the nucleus of a future economic studies faculty. In 1965, the University of Havana upgraded economic studies by taking it out of the faculty of humanities and creating a separate institute of economy (*Instituto de Economía*).

This extensive initial effort in higher economic studies suggests that enrollments probably increased in the first half of the 1960s. They probably dropped only in the decade's second half, as economic studies was downgraded. In 1967, for example, courses in the political economy of socialism were abolished. The discipline of accounting was looked down upon, and its name was changed to "economic control," to eliminate any commercial connotation. Many textbooks were jettisoned, often replaced by the political pronouncements of revolutionary leaders.

In the late 1960s, the Cuban leadership, like such Marxists of an earlier generation as Nikolai Bukharin and Rosa Luxemburg, came to view economics as a science of bourgeois society that had lost its relevance with the advent of socialism.[21] In 1970, then-President Osvaldo Dorticós described the prevailing attitude among his fellow revolutionary leaders in the late 1960s: Although it had always been recognized, he stated, that to be an engineer, architect, or medical doctor required formal training, it had been widely believed that economic and administrative posts required nothing more than revolutionary consciousness and personal experience on the job.[22] Such an attitude directly led to the rise of politically reliable but formally untrained economic administrators. It also easily led to a devaluation of economic studies and a drop of enrollments in this area.

In the 1960s, then, the revolutionary leadership confronted the supply side of the skill problem by dramatically expanding and transforming all levels of the educational system. But, although educational progress was impressive in this period, a variety of problems remained, and by the end of the decade many earlier advances were eroding. As will be seen in Chapter 5, educational progress in the 1960s failed to fully compensate for the drain of skills through the exodus of intermediate-level personnel out of the country. By the end of the 1960s the skill problem, although mitigated to some extent, remained severe. As a result, throughout the 1960s the revolutionary leadership searched for ways to minimize the need for many, especially administrative, skills.

Minimizing the Demand for Skills

From 1962 to 1965, Cuban revolutionaries engaged in a so-called Great Debate. This dispute had many facets and ranged over such issues as Marxist theory on the socialist transition, the nature of socialist and communist morality, and even the nature of the human species. In immediate practical terms, the antagonists in this debate argued for the exclusive use of one of two organizational and motivational models.[23]

One, commonly called the "auto-finance" system and adapted from the reform models of the Soviet bloc, operated at the time in the Cuban agricultural sector. This system decentralized many economic decisions down to the enterprises, which served as semi-autonomous centers of production, resource allocation, accounting, and profit realization. The activities of these enterprises were coordinated through a combination of central planning and market mechanisms, and their workers were motivated primarily by personal and material incentives.

The other mechanism then operated in the Cuban industrial sector, and was called the "centralized budgetary" system. This system sought to centralize economic decisions, and to relieve enterprises of autonomy. The activities of enterprises were coordinated, not at all by market mechanisms, but totally by central planning and budgetary controls. Workers in this system were to be motivated by personal material incentives to fulfill production quotas, but only moral incentives would be offered for overfulfillment. Although personal material incentives would be offered, collective and moral incentives would predominate and as quickly as possible replace personal material ones altogether.

As Guevara, the leading proponent of the centralized budgetary model, made clear, each side in the Great Debate argued that its own model would more successfully minimize the demand for skills by requiring a smaller administrative apparatus and fewer trained personnel to operate it. When the proponents of the auto-finance system claimed that his centralized budgetary model suffered from "a tendency toward bureaucracy," Guevara countered:

> One point must therefore be constantly stressed: The entire administrative apparatus must be organized on a rational basis. Now, from the standpoint of objective analysis, it is obvious that there will be less bureaucracy the more centralized are enterprises or production units recording and controlling operations. If every enterprise could centralize all its administrative activities, its bureaucracy would be reduced to a small nucleus of unit directors plus someone to collect information for headquarters.[24]

Guevara was well aware that, to the extent it was implemented in the industrial sector, his model never operated in this lean, well-organized fashion. He complained in 1963, for example, that "a goodly number of civil servants put in requests for more personnel as their only means of carrying out a task otherwise quite easily solved by a little brain power."[25] This tendency to bloat the administrative apparatus doubtless stemmed in part from the fact that many members of the apparatus, appointed for political more than educational credentials, while professional revolutionaries, were still amateur administrators. But Guevara still maintained that his model was the best designed to compensate for the skill problem, so long as the administrative apparatus was strictly organized.

During the Great Debate, Fidel Castro never took a public

position on which organizational and motivational model should be preferred. But as the debate subsided in 1965 and major theoretical journals were shut down—the order of the day was to produce, not debate—a third, the aforementioned *fidelista* model, was imposed on the economy. Along with unique features of its own, this model eclectically combined elements from both the auto-finance and centralized budgetary models.

According to some scholars, the imposition of the *fidelista* model in the late 1960s was a movement toward greater decentralization; according to others, it was a movement toward greater centralization.[26] Both are accurate, but each only with respect to particular aspects of the system. Certainly the power to make decisions affecting the whole society, the most dramatic example being the 10-million-ton sugar goal for 1970, remained concentrated in the hands of the revolutionary leadership. Only the implementation of such decisions was decentralized.

This led to many different local solutions or near-solutions and, from a societal point of view, much chaos. When decisions were not satisfactorily implemented, however, especially when this involved an economic area considered critical, the revolutionary leadership often intervened to impose its own plan for implementation at the base. Intervention often took place through the Communist Party or the Revolutionary Armed Forces, which led some commentators to speak of growing centralization of power and militarization in this period. Thus, depending on which aspect of this movement one cares to emphasize, it can be viewed as a movement either toward decentralization or toward centralization. In fact, it was an historically specific combination of both.

Like the auto-finance model, the *fidelista* model allowed enterprises to operate semi-autonomously, but without either effective central or market coordination. In late 1965, for example, revolutionary leaders abolished the ministry of finance and reduced the power of the national bank. In 1966, they weakened the central planning board (*Junta Central de Planificación*–JUCEPLAN), which had directed all macroeconomic plans. They also adopted regional and local mini-plans, without coherently connecting them. The leaders provided for the decentralized allocation of resources, but without using market mechanisms. In 1967, they abolished all payments and receipts in state enterprises, all taxes, and all interest on bank credits. By 1968, they stopped preparing a national budget for the entire economy.

With Guevara and other proponents of the centralized budgetary model, the adherents of the *fidelista* model shared an emphasis on the importance of using moral incentives to create a "new man" (and by implication a "new woman") who would unselfishly sacrifice for the common good.[27] Whatever broader philosophical notions underlay this view, both Guevara and supporters of the *fidelista* model considered the need for a "new person" to be based in revolutionary Cuba's material reality; Cuba, they insisted, was simply too poor to rely primarily on personal material incentives. As Fidel Castro later explained, "(Our) poor countries ... have very little to give on the material level. If they want to give goods they can't, and if they convert material goods into the main motivation they fail."[28]

Moreover, having radically redistributed wealth and income and introduced a host of egalitarian measures that seriously weakened the incentive structure of capitalism, with its promise of personal material gain and threat of unemployment, Guevara and the adherents of the *fidelista* model felt compelled to find collective and moral motivations for work.

Lastly, high rates of capital formation and labor-intensive

growth projects were deemed necessary to develop the material base of the future society. A "new person" who would work long and hard not for personal advantage but for the good of the community was seen as the ideal in acheiving these. Although everyone would benefit from enormously expanded opportunities for collective consumption (e.g., free health and educational services), for the sake of economic development, the "new person's" wants and personal consumption would have to remain austere. Guevara and the proponents of the *fidelista* model, in short, considered the "new person" the precondition for economic advance in revolutionary Cuba.

When supporters of the *fidelista* model were not simply assuming that the "new person" already universally existed, they utilized a host of mechanisms, from egalitarian distribution and moral rewards to voluntary labor and ideological exhortation, to create such persons. But unlike Guevara, they never seem to have given much thought to the organizational prerequisites for the development of the "new person."

Rightly or wrongly, Guevara argued that only his highly centralized and rationalized model could accomplish the task. Without centralization, the economy would be fractured into a multitude of competing interests which would undercut collective consciousness. His model aimed at eliminating capitalist market relations among production units and shortly thereafter eliminating personal material incentives for individual workers. From there it sought to construct a unified economic organization to make each individual feel part of a single social whole to which he or she could relate with a profound collective consciousness. A truly collective and rationally organized economic structure was needed to form the objective basis of the subjective collective sense.[29]

At least in intention, Guevara approached the creation of a

"new person" practically. The adherents of the *fidelista* model, as will be shown presently, approached the question idealistically.

Instead of strictly organizing the administrative apparatus in accordance with either the auto-finance or centralized budgetary models, the backers of the *fidelista* model radically shook it up and reduced its size. In one of their central documents, a series of editorials in the Communist Party daily *Granma* during May 1967,[30] the revolutionary leadership declared an "antibureaucratic revolution," a campaign which recalled earlier efforts in 1964 but which this time was to cut wider and deeper.

The proponents of the *fidelista* model now attempted to pare the administrative apparatus to a minimum. They frequently rotated administrative personnel to prevent the "tendency to settle in and consider oneself 'indispensable.'" They sent administrative cadres out of their offices to deal with production problems on the spot rather than sit behind their desks and shuffle papers. Fewer administrative personnel, fewer rules to be imposed on production units, less information and fewer forms to be sent up and down the administrative apparatus, less red tape altogether—these were the goals of the antibureaucratic revolution.

With fewer administrative controls over lower levels, fewer administrative controllers were needed, and administrative personnel were often required to engage in "productive"—that is, manual—labor. In the *fidelista* period, Fidel Castro himself posed for an occasional snapshot, decked out in worker's mufti, swinging a machete among the sugar stalks.[31]

In response to the scarcity of administrative skills, then, the supporters of the *fidelista* model pushed for a lean organizational structure—even more radically than did the proponents of the auto-finance and centralized budgetary models. The backers of the *fidelista* model, however, did not attempt to compensate for scarce skills through rational organization. Rather, at least in the temporary period when the overriding goal was the production of 10 million tons of sugar, they tended to deny the usefulness of such skills.

This denial in part stemmed from the pressures of their own goal of 10 million tons of sugar. As problems emerged in realizing this goal, the adherents of the *fidelista* model pushed all the harder and attempted to mobilize all available labor to meet the goal. They apparently concluded that what was needed was not skills but individuals willing to callous their hands. The political consciousness of the political cadres and of the other "new people" would compensate for scarce skills.

But this bias also stemmed from the widespread view that many in the prerevolutionary intermediate social strata were politically unreliable. This perception had already fueled the discrimination, described in the last chapter, against many in the intermediate level. Now this perception was projected wholesale onto many intermediate-level occupations, regardless of the social origins of their incumbents. Together, the *fidelista* "revolutionary offensive" against the small proprietor sector and the *fidelista* model with its antibureaucratic revolution marked the zenith of discrimination against Cuba's prerevolutionary intermediate social strata.

Denying the usefulness of many administrative skills, the adherents of the *fidelista* model failed to use even the skills available, and they forced many administrative personnel directly into production. They also failed, as seen in the last section, to create many new skills they could have used. And most important for future developments, they pushed to an extreme the practice of appointing administrative personnel on the basis of political rather than educational credentials. As will be seen in Chapter 5, despite their few skills and often inefficient work styles, these political cadres would retain administrative posts for a long time to come.

The Crisis of 1970

A few key economic indicators illustrate the overall results of the *fidelista* implementation of the second development strategy. Although this strategy envisioned a 14 percent annual growth rate through 1970, in 1975 Fidel Castro stated that the actual rate had been only 4 percent.[32] Outside commentators typically have put the rate even lower: Claes Brundenius, for example, has given estimates from which it can be computed that, from 1966 through 1970, total material product grew at an average annual rate of 3.72 percent, gross domestic product at .68 percent, while gross domestic product per capita fell at an average annual rate of 1.14 percent.[33] Moreover, although a record 8.5 million tons of sugar were produced in 1970, this fell short of the 10-million-ton goal and continued the pattern of sugar shortfalls that had begun in 1966. Sugar production was never less than 15 percent below plan between 1966 and 1970, and in 1969 it fell a full 50 percent below.[34]

Even with this, the attempt to reach the 10-million-ton goal diverted resources to the sugar sector and starved many nonsugar operations. In 1970, steel deliveries were 38 percent below plan, soap production 32 percent, and butter production 33 percent. In addition, production of liquid milk, vegetables, root crops, beans, meat, and poultry in 1970 all fell below 1969 levels. In 1970, the record gains in sugar production were probably outpaced by losses in the rest of the economy.[35]

The *fidelista* model, with its weakened central controls and mini-plans, led to the waste of many resources, a loss that had not just economic but also political consequences: It helped undercut the "new person" strategy of developing collective consciousness.

As the revolutionary leadership pushed the investment rate to new heights, personal consumption, although equalized through rationing and cushioned by expanded collective consumption, was generally depressed. In 1970, for example, daily per capita calorie intake averaged 2,565, almost 400 calories short of the 2,940 considered necessary for the average Cuban; and daily per capita protein intake averaged 68.8, about twenty grams fewer than the necessary eighty-nine.[36]

Encouraged to work long and hard while suffering low levels of personal consumption, even the most committed "new person" could become disillusioned when effort and sacrifice did not result in promised economic results. By wasting material and human resources, the revolutionary leadership was wasting the people's labor. Willingness to sacrifice, revolutionary enthusiasm, collective consciousness— all the key elements of the *fidelista* model were used recklessly.

The operation of the *fidelista* system of labor mobilization and incentives makes this very clear. In the late 1960s, massive numbers of individuals were mobilized for voluntary labor, a practice intended to instill "new person" attitudes. Such voluntary labor took several forms. Sometimes workers would volunteer to work without pay after their regular jobs, on weekends, or on holidays. Sometimes whole production units would commit themselves to voluntary labor. Some of their number would go off to the sugar fields, for example, while being paid their regular wages, and their remaining co-workers would compensate for their absence with more intensive labor or unpaid overtime. Sometimes housewives or others not in the regular labor force would volunteer for unpaid work.

Regardless of its form, much voluntary labor was irrationally used. In the *fidelista* period, its success was typically judged by the number of hours worked, whatever its output. Stories abound of volunteers transported to projects that were either ill-conceived, poorly organized, or lacking in necessary tools and materials. Productivity on many projects was extremely low, or could not make up in output value enough to cover transport and fuel costs. As a result, many projects produced little more than lessened morale for their participants.[37]

Regular paid labor was also affected by the *fidelista* incentive system, with its emphasis on moral over material incentives. Work norms, for example, which had been instituted in 1961, fell into disuse after 1966. Between 1961 and 1966 wages were cut by the amount that output quotas were unmet, and bonuses were paid at the rate of 50 percent of the amount by which quotas were exceeded. But after 1966 workers were seldom materially penalized for not reaching quotas, and it became a sign of revolutionary commitment to forego bonuses. According to then-Minister of Labor Jorge Risquet:

> Even though legally in force fines, suspensions, etc., are typically capitalist sanctions ... and we have refrained from imposing them. ... Sanctions must be the last resort. Education and reeducation through collective self-criticism and the help of other workers are the basic weapons in this struggle.[38]

Thus to develop the "new person," "capitalist sanctions," that is, material incentives, were replaced with moral ones.

This is not to say, however, that material incentives disappeared altogether. Regular work was still remunerated through wages, with different wage levels for different types of work. Like all socialist incentive systems, the *fidelista* system was mixed. Official wage scales were only slightly differentiated and such inequalities as did occur from wage differences were mitigated by rationing at set prices and free services. Nevertheless, significant inequalities arose from the actual wage. The policy of the revolutionary leadership was to equalize wages from the bottom up, not from the top down, as productivity increases made this possible.[39] This meant that so-called historical wages, that is, wage levels carried over from the pre-revolutionary past, would be eliminated very slowly, and mostly through attrition. During his 1967 trip to the Nicaro Nickel Plant, K.S. Karol found engineers earning historical wages up to 1,700 pesos per month, while new engineers working under official wage scales were earning from 300 to 400 pesos per month, and average production workers made only 100 pesos per month.[40]

Such widely divergent pay for similar work, however, did not always result from historical wages. Other out-of-line wages, as they were called, derived not from the capitalist past but from the administrative inefficiencies of the revolutionary present. Because of incorrect evaluation, work requiring fewer skills or less effort was often relatively over-remunerated in comparison to work requiring more skills or more effort. Also, as production units were merged or otherwise rationalized, and particular jobs eliminated or transformed, workers whose jobs became less demanding were often paid at their old higher wage, while new workers were paid according to the lower official scales. Even workers who voluntarily transferred to less demanding jobs continued to receive their old wages. How widespread such inequities were is hard to judge, but, according to one Cuban official, they still affected "a significant percentage ... of Cuban workers as late as 1975."[41]

Especially since these inequalities and inequities often affected workers doing the same work in the same plant, they undoubtedly took their toll in lessened collective consciousness. The efficacy of moral incentives would seem to depend on, among other things, considerable equality and equity in the sphere of material incentives. A "new person" morality would be unlikely to develop fully when individuals see their sacrifices for the collectivity benefitting others more than themselves.

The material side of the *fidelista* incentive mix also undercut the development of collective consciousness by generating excess consumer liquidity, or incomes that outpaced available goods. After 1965, massive investments were made in agriculture, especially for future sugar output, and in cattle breeding. Such investments would result in increased output only over the long term. Investments were also heavy in collectively consumed services such as education, which was free and which would not pay off in increased output for many years. In addition, since most voluntary labor was paid at regular wages regardless of productivity, the sugar harvest, which used a considerable number of inexperienced volunteers, helped generate excess consumer liquidity. With prices held more or less constant, workers made considerably more money than there were goods or services on which to spend it.

If workers could not use their money for goods, many of them exchanged it for leisure, either by absenteeism or by low productivity on the job. In 1969, for example, the rate of absenteeism never fell below 35 percent for permanent farm workers in Camagüey province. At the peak of the 1970 harvest, the final test of the "new person," the absentee rate for the whole economy reached 29 percent. In 1969, Leo Huberman and Paul Sweezy estimated that the agricultural labor force was utilized at somewhere around "50 percent of practicable capacity."[42]

The extent to which these problems resulted directly from the inadequate planning and administrative procedures of the *fidelista* model is impossible to judge. But it seems reasonable to suppose that excess consumer liquidity and lack of a rational system of material sanctions and bonuses, both of which prevented harder work from paying off in increased personal consumption, played a significant role. Collective consciousness was developing unevenly: as many individuals made an effort to meet the leadership's goals and demands, others' work diminished. The fact that by 1968 voluntary work accounted for 8 to 10 percent of all labor indicated the efforts of some.[43] Absenteeism and low productivity indicated the backsliding of others.

In 1970, Fidel Castro pointed out the extent to which tension among workers had been engendered by division between those who were expending great effort and those who were not. He remarked: "Go to any factory and ask the workers what should be done about the lazy ones, the ones who don't work. If you don't watch out, they'll go so far as to demand that they be shot."[44]

Given the regime's own mistakes, which surely demoralized many a devoted worker, accusing others of being "lazy ones" (*vagos*) could be considered blaming the victims. Be that as it may, the imbalanced incentive system, by allowing "lazy ones" to effectively live off the labor of others, generated resentments in the working class that further eroded the ability of collective and moral incentives to create greater collective consciousness. The *fidelista* incentive system undermined rather than encouraged the development of many "new persons."

Even beyond the tensions it engendered among workers, the *fidelista* implementation of the second development strategy eventually generated tensions between the revolutionary leadership and its political supporters in the working class. Workers could hardly fail to note that, through no fault of their own, much of their labor was being wasted. Many administrative personnel, on the other hand, did not recognize this. Instead, as a 1969 government report made clear, they tended to blame workers and took excessively coercive action against many of them.[45] This could only have added to the workers' resentment and further strained relations between the leadership and its political base.

Further aggravating tensions, in this period workers lacked institutionalized means for making suggestions, registering complaints, and venting resentments. Labor volunteers, for example, had little say about how their work was organized and few means to criticize the inefficient organizers of their projects. In regular workplaces, a few exemplary individuals who had been designated "vanguard workers" often made decisions for their coworkers.

The *fidelista* anti-bureaucratic revolution had cut into the organizational apparatus of the unions. The number of national unions dropped by almost half, down to fourteen, while their provincial and municipal branches were eliminated, and unions across the board lost many of their former functions.[46] In the *fidelista* period, as Maurice Zeitlin put it, Cuban unions virtually "withered away."[47]

In addition, in this period the Communist Party virtually took over the functions and organization of the state. It involved itself in the running of everything from the Academy of Sciences to the local grocery store. Enmeshed in day-to-day operations, the party could not properly analyze problems and develop effective solutions. Because it had become the administration itself, it lost the all-important political vantage point of supervising and guiding the administration—uncovering its mistakes to make sure that it serves the interests of the Cuban people.[48]

To be sure, the Cuban people could make their voices heard in the *fidelista* period. They could, after all, speak directly with the revolutionary leadership, especially Fidel Castro, who commonly mixed with them, queried them, listened to their criticisms, and then translated these into policy.[49] But given the uneven and episodic character of this sort of political partici- pation, it is not surprising that increasing numbers of workers resorted to other mechanisms, once described by Che Guevara:

> The state at times makes mistakes. When this occurs, the collective enthusiasm diminishes palpably as a result of the quantitative diminishing that takes place in each of the elements that make up the collective, and work becomes paralyzed until it finally shrinks to insignificant proportions: this is the time to rectify.[50]

Thus, in 1970 the Cuban revolution had reached a critical turning point. The advance of education had been impressive, but insufficient to adequately address the skill problem; the *fidelista* implementation of the second economic develop- ment strategy had failed to deliver the promised economic results. As a result, by 1970 the relationship between the revolutionary leadership and its popular political base showed definite signs of strain. The administrative apparatus, more- over, was in shambles; it was filled with political cadres who were possibly professional revolutionaries but, with less than six years of education on average, definitely amateur admin- istrators. As will be seen in Chapter 5, many of these political cadres, with their few skills and inefficient work styles, would retain administrative posts well into the future.

Notes

1. For good analyses of this first strategy and its failings, see Arthur MacEwan, *Revolution and Economic Development in Cuba* (New York: St. Martin's Press, 1981); and Archibald R.M. Ritter, *The Economic Development of Revolutionary Cuba* (New York: Praeger, 1974).
2. For an excellent discussion of U.S. economic warfare against Cuba in this period, see Morris H. Morley, *Imperial State and*

Revolution: The United States and Cuba, 1952-1986 (Cambridge: Cambridge University Press, 1987), esp. chap. 5.

3. For full discussions of this second strategy, see ibid. and Heinrich Brunner, *Cuban Sugar Policy from 1963 to 1970* (Pittsburgh: University of Pittsburgh Press, 1977).

4. MacEwan, *Revolution and Economic Development*, chaps. 13-21, however, makes a strong argument for a more positive evaluation of this second strategy.

5. For good overviews of the literacy campaign, see Richard Fagen, *The Transformation of Political Culture in Cuba* (Stanford: Stanford University Press, 1969); Michel Huteau and Jacques Lautrey, *L'Éducation à Cuba* (Paris: François Maspero, 1973).

6. MacEwan, *Revolution and Economic Development*, pp. 77-78.

7. Adult education in Cuba extends through the secondary level, and its graduates may go on to higher education while continuing in their regular jobs. Regular education begins with an extensive system of preprimary education. This is followed by an elementary education system of six years (four years before the revolution) and a secondary education system of up to eight years. After elementary school, students may enter one of three tracks of the basic secondary system: One track leads directly to employment and continued secondary education in the adult system. Another track leads to a polytechnical school for two or three years and then to a job coupled with adult education. The third track leads to three years of study in a basic secondary school. Graduates of the latter schools may enter one of several tracks in the advanced secondary system: One track leads to employment and adult education at the advanced secondary level. Another track leads to a polytechnical institute, either directly or after two or three years of study in an advanced polytechnical school, and then to higher education along with a regular job. Another track leads to three years in a preuniversity and then either directly to higher education or to two years in a polytechnical institute and then either to employment or higher education. For a simplified flow chart of the Cuban educational system, see Francisco Ferreira Báez, "El sistema de formación professional de nivel medio en Cuba," in Haydée

García and Hans Blumenthal (eds.), *Formación profesional en Latinoamérica* (Caracas: Editorial Nueva Sociedad, 1987), p. 115.
8. Reported by Carmelo Mesa-Lago, *The Economy of Socialist Cuba* (Albuquerque: University of New Mexico Press, 1981), p. 164. Although changes in statistical methodology might have accounted for some of this increase, it probably did not account for all of it.
9. Ministerio de Educación, *El plan de perfeccionamiento y desarrollo del Sistema Nacional de Educación de Cuba* (Havana, 1976).
10. Ministerio de Educación, *Informe a la Asamblea Nacional del Poder Popular* (Havana 1981), pp. 344–47.
11. Consejo Superior de Universidades, *La reforma de la enseñanza superior de Cuba* (1962).
12. Concepción Duchesne, "Incremento y desarrollo en la educación superior, 1976–1980," *Bohemia*, 28 November 1980, p. 36. I use the term "higher education centers" because, according to current Cuban nomenclature, the higher education system is made up of universities and the smaller and more specialized university centers and superior institutes. For a graphic representation of Cuba's higher education system, see Nikolai Kolesnikov, *Cuba: educación popular y preparación de los cuadros nacionales, 1959–1982* (Moscow: Editorial Progreso, 1983), Anexo, Esquema 13.
13. For a detailed description of the ideological struggle in highei education written from a counterrevolutionary perspective, see Jaime Suchlicki, *University Students and Revolution in Cuba, 1920–1968* (Coral Gables, FL: University of Miami Press, 1968), chap. 5.
14. See "Estudio preliminar sobre algunos factores que inciden en las realizaciones docentes de los alumnos de primer año," *Sobre Educación Superior* (1971), pp. 43–50; and Guillermo Aria and Arturo Bas, "Construcción de un instrumento adecuado para evaluar a los estudiantes que ingresar a la universidad," *Sobre Educación Superior* (1971), pp. 51–65.
15. Author's interviews BFGO1.81 and BFGO2.81.
16. Consejo Superior de Universidades, *La reforma.*
17. Depending on the context, I have translated the Spanish term

economía either as "economy" or as "economic studies" instead of "economics." I have also used the term "economic professionals" to refer to professional economists (*economistas*) but not solely to them. The reason for these choices is that the distinction between economic studies and what in the United States would be called business studies is less complete in Cuba than it is in the United States. Cuban economic studies programs, for example, commonly train not just professional economists but also accountants, managers, etc. Moreover, all economic professionals in Cuba, even those who are not professional economists, are eligible to join the National Association of Cuban Economic Professionals (*Asociación Nacional de Economistas de Cuba*). It makes sense, then, to speak of economic professionals in Cuba as a single category.

18. Author's interview ST.80.
19. See, for example, Ministerio de Educación, *Informe de la delegación de la República de Cuba a la VII Conferencia de Ministros de Educación Superior y Media Especializada de los Países Socialistas* (Havana: 1972), p. 82.
20. Unless otherwise indicated, the information in this chapter on Cuba's economic professionals is from Alexis Codina Jiménez and Joaquín Fernández, "Apuntes en el XX aniversario del inicio de la formación de economistas," *Economía y Desarrollo* 71 (November/December 1982): 11–37.
21. Nikolai Bukharin, *The Economics of the Transformation Period* (New York: Bergman, 1971); Rosa Luxemburg, "What is Economics?" in Mary-Alice Waters (ed.), *Rosa Luxemburg Speaks* (New York: Pathfinder Press, 1970), pp. 219–45.
22. Osvaldo Dorticós, "Formación de cuadros económicos-administrativos en la industria ligera," *Economía y Desarrollo* 4 (October/December 1970): 3–8.
23. For this debate and the economic models it counterposed, see the collection by Bertram Silverman (ed.), *Man and Socialism in Cuba: The Great Debate* (New York: Atheneum, 1973).
24. Ernesto "Che" Guevara, "On the Budgetary Finance System," in ibid., p. 152.
25. Ernesto "Che" Guevara, "Against Bureaucratism," in John

Gerassi (ed.), *Venceremos! The Speeches and Writings of Che Guevara* (New York: Simon and Schuster, 1968), p. 224.

26. For examples of these two positions, see respectively Nelson P. Valdés, "The Cuban Revolution: Economic Organization and Bureaucracy," *Latin American Perspectives* 20 (Winter 1979): 13-37; and René Dumont, *Is Cuba Socialist?* (New York: Viking Press, 1974).

27. Perhaps the most representative statements are Ernesto "Che" Guevara, "Man and Socialism in Cuba," in Silverman, *Man and Socialism in Cuba*, pp. 337-354; and Fidel Castro, "We Will Never Build a Communist Consciousness with a Dollar Sign in the Minds and Hearts of Men," in Martin Kenner and James Petras (eds.), *Fidel Castro Speaks* (New York: Grove Press, 1969), pp. 199-213.

28. Fidel Castro, *Fidel in Chile* (New York: International Publishers, 1975), p. 185.

29. For a corroborating interpretation of Guevara's thought, see Carlos Tablada, *Che Guevara: Economics and Politics in the Transition to Socialism* (Sydney, Australia: Pathfinder/Pacific and Asia, 1989).

30. "The Struggle Against Bureaucracy: A Decisive Task," in Michael Taber (ed.), *Fidel Castro Speeches, Vol. 2: Our Power is That of the Working People* (New York: Pathfinder Press, 1983), pp. 68-90.

31. As, for example, on the cover of the paperback edition of K.S. Karol, *Guerrillas in Power: The Course of the Cuban Revolution* (New York: Hill and Wang, 1970).

32. The planned rate was given by Carlos Rafael Rodrìguez, cited in Ritter, *Economic Development of Revolutionary Cuba*, p. 316; Fidel Castro gave the actual rate in his *Main Report to the First Congress of the Communist Party of Cuba* (Havana: Communist Party of Cuba, 1977).

33. Author's computations based on Claes Brundenius, *Revolutionary Cuba: The Challenge of Economic Growth with Equity* (Boulder, CO: Westview Press, 1984), p. 40; see also Andrew Zimbalist and Claes Brundenius, *The Cuban Economy: Measurement and Analysis of Socialist Performance* (Baltimore: The Johns Hopkins Press, 1989).

34. MacEwan, *Revolution and Economic Development*, p. 117.

35. Ritter, *Economic Development of Revolutionary Cuba*, pp. 183–87.
36. Data supplied in 1981 by Eugenio Balari, Director of the Cuban Institute of Internal Demand.
37. Ritter, *Economic Development of Revolutionary Cuba*, pp. 287–88. Also see the complaints of the *Cubano de Acero* factory workers reported in *Granma Weekly Review*, 2 September 1973.
38. Quoted in Maurice Zeitlin, *Revolutionary Politics and the Cuban Working Class* (New York: Harper and Row, 1970), p. xxxii.
39. See the remarks of Fidel Castro in Martin Kenner and James Petras, *Fidel Castro Speaks*, p. 288; and Karol, *Guerrillas in Power*, p. 343.
40. Karol, *Guerrillas in Power*, p. 338.
41. Eduardo DeLlano, "Wages under Socialism," *Granma Weekly Review*, 25 November 1973.
42. Leo Huberman and Paul Sweezy, *Socialism in Cuba* (New York: Monthly Review Press, 1969), p. 143.
43. Carmelo Mesa-Lago, "Economic Significance of Unpaid Labor in Socialist Cuba," *Industrial and Labor Relations Review* 22 (April 1969): 339-57.
44. Fidel Castro, "Report on the Cuban Economy," in Rolando Bonachea and Nelson Valdés (eds.), *Cuba in Revolution* (Garden City, New York: Doubleday, 1972), p. 341.
45. *Granma Weekly Review*, 9 November 1969.
46. Linda Fuller, "The Politics of Workers' Control in Cuba, 1959–1983: The Work Center and the National Arena" (Ph.D. diss, University of California at Berkeley, 1985), pp. 134–36; also, by the same author, see *Work and Democracy in Socialist Cuba* (Philadelphia: Temple University Press, 1992), esp. chap. 3.
47. Zeitlin, *Revolutionary Politics and the Cuban Working Class*, p. xxv.
48. See the discussion of these points in Lourdes Casal, "Cuban Communist Party: The Best Among the Good," *Cuba Review* 6, no. 3 (September 1976): 24.
49. For vivid illustrations of this political process, see Lee Lockwood, *Castro's Cuba, Cuba's Fidel* (New York: Vintage Books, 1969).
50. Guevara, "Man and Socialism in Cuba," pp. 339–40.

Chapter 4

The Post-1970 Rectification and the New Professionals

After 1970, Cuban socialism went through a profound rectification process, designed to overcome the strains of the late 1960s and to resolidify the revolution's popular base.[1] The revolutionary leadership accelerated the upgrading of the population's skills with an even more rapid expansion of education.

The leadership replaced the *fidelista* system with more balanced incentives and with new organizational structures and operating procedures. A new development strategy was introduced that pursued less ambitious economic goals, and that again emphasized industry over agriculture. Between 1976 and 1980, for example, industry took 35 percent of Cuban investments, while agriculture took less than 20 percent.[2]

Although the post-1970 rectification did not, as some claimed, amount to a wholesale "Sovietization" of Cuban socialism,[3] it did result in Cuba integrating economically with the Soviet bloc and borrowing significantly from contemporary Soviet practice.

New organizational principles were introduced after 1970 that would usher in a transformation of Cuba's administrative personnel. These principles called for formally educating or replacing the political cadres who had risen to intermediate-level posts on the basis of political credentials in the 1960s. Entering a decline, they were seen more and more as the *old* political cadres, or simply the old cadres, as they will be referred to in the rest of this work.

Furthermore, the new organizational principles in effect called for an increasing number of formally trained personnel, that is, of new professionals. These new professionals would be supplied by a dramatic expansion of education, especially at the secondary and higher levels. The minimum qualification for entry into intermediate-level occupations became a secondary school degree.

Institutionalizing Democratic Centralism

The post-1970 rectification process partly aimed at institutionalizing new organizational structures, with differentiated areas and levels of responsibility. The major economic and political organizations—such as the enterprises, trade unions, and popular assemblies—were given formally delineated spheres of responsibility, as were the hierarchy of levels within these organizations. Although akin to Max Weber's ideal-typical rational bureaucracy, this new organizational setup did not operate solely along the monocratic, non-democratic lines of Weber's model.[4] Instead, its operating procedures encompassed an element of bottom-up participation. Adapted in part from Soviet models, these new structures were supposed to operate according to a three-step process for making and implementing decisions, along democratic centralist lines.[5]

In the first step of this process, the issue or problem at hand was to be collectively discussed. Here, intermediate-level personnel and, at the local level, the general population were to be involved in analyzing problems and in examining and proposing possible solutions. Failure to adequately carry through this step was said to lead to less than optimal decisions—in that such decisions would ignore realities of which only lower bodies could have full knowledge; and to bureau-cratic centralist decisions—in that lower bodies would not identify with such decisions, which would then have to be imposed from above.

In the second step of the democratic centralist process a decision was to be made. This responsibility was assigned to leaders of enterprises, of work centers (local subunits of enterprises), of mass organizations, or of higher party and state organs. More general or more important decisions were to be made by higher-level leaders, while less general or less import-ant decisions were to be reserved for lower-level leaders. Allowing decisions to be made at too low a level was said to lead to local improvisation, waste of resources, and inattention to internal and external factors beyond the purview of lower bodies, or, in short, to less than optimal decisions. Allowing decisions to be made at too high a level was called bureaucratic centralism, in that the higher levels would be usurping the responsibilities of lower-level leaders.

In the third step, the active participation of the lower levels, down to the localities, was to be elicited in the implementation and control of decisions, that is, in ensuring that they were carried out fully and correctly according to plan. Participation was to be encouraged through persuasion, most especially through fully explaining the rationale for the particular deci-sions made. Failure to elicit lower level participation through persuasion and explanation was dubbed a bureaucratic cen-tralist error, in that lower level compliance and cooperation would then have to be commanded from above.

These principles defined, however generally, a particular distribution of decision-making power, one that pointed to the increased importance of the new professionals. First, the prin-ciples stipulated that the most general or important decisions should be made centrally, that is, by the revolutionary leadership. But, although the leadership reserved ultimate decision-making responsibility for itself, this did not preclude it from eliciting the advice of trained specialists from among the new professionals.

Second, insofar as the principles were based on the assumptions of democratic centralism, people at the local level could not make decisions, but could and were expected to participate in the pre-decision-making stage of discussion and in the post-decision-making stage of implementation. Democratic centralism thus envisioned eliciting and solidifying popular support for decisions made at higher levels through participatory mechanisms, however limited.

Third, these principles stipulated that less general or less important decisions should be left to lower-level personnel. If decisions made at this level were to be optimal, lower-level decision makers, of course, had to possess skills adequate to their responsibilities. On this basis, citing democratic centralism, the leadership demanded and argued for the replacement of old cadres by new professionals.

In implementing democratic centralist principles, then, the leadership defined the new distribution of decision-making power. These principles served to justify both the subordination of the new professionals to the leadership and the rise of the new professionals to replace the old cadres. In addition, the new professionals received a clear and stable intermediate-level role in the rectified organizational structures. Finally, democratic centralist reorganization brought with it the demand for limited popular participation and training of more new professionals.

Rectifying Economic Organization and Incentives

Among the first organizational structures to be institution-alized according to the principles of democratic centralism after 1970 were the trade unions, which, as already noted, had virtually withered away in the late 1960s. From 1970 to 1972, the unions were reorganized into twenty-three national unions in the various sectors of the economy, and were equipped with the provincial and municipal organizational levels that had been stripped away in 1966.[6] This reconstruction of the trade unions culminated in the Thirteenth Congress of the Central Organization of Cuban Trade Unions (CTC), held in 1973.

Among other things, this congress clarified the role of the unions. As mass organizations to which all workers could belong, the unions would be considered separate from both party and state. The division between the unions and the party, however, would be functional rather than political. Unions were to function, in the typical communist metaphor, as "transmission belts," both up and down, between the party and the mass of workers. Because workers constitute only a part of the population, their unions were not empowered to control the management of the economy. Rather, they were expected to follow the ideological lead of the party, as the vanguard organization of the whole society. Yet as one labor leader put it: "The trade unions are not going every day to the party to ask what has to be done. Their function is to develop, along the fundamentals of the party line, the administration of the trade unions."[7]

This partial separation of the responsibilities of the unions from those of the party and the state marked a change. It paved the way for the differentiation of the functions of the unions and the enterprise and work center (local subunits of enter-prises) management, however vague the actual power dele-

gated to the unions. As the organizational voice of the particular interests of the workers, the unions were now expected
to point out errors in the work and planning process and to
help organize workers' participation; workers were to be
involved in discussing the basic production issues and in
controlling the implementation of the economic plan of their
enterprise and work center.

The Thirteenth CTC Congress approved regular
worker/management assemblies, collective worker/manage-
ment work commitments, and enterprise and work center
councils on which union representatives would sit with managers, technical personnel, and party representatives. Even
though managers would continue to be considered ultimately
responsible for the overall performance of their economic unit,
union representatives were not to indiscriminately take
management's side, as many had in the past. Managers would
still be appointed from above, and workers were given no
formal authority to remove managers, but the Cuban workers
interviewed by Linda Fuller in 1982 and 1983 "expressed
confidence that they could have a decisive hand in the
dismissal of an administrator" through their union.[8]

As the statutes approved by the Thirteenth CTC Congress
summed it up, the trade unions were to play a counterpart or,
perhaps more accurately, a countervailing role (*un papel
contrapartida*) to management. This included actively criticizing all manifestations of managerial inefficiency, as well as
protecting workers' rights.[9]

Another major accomplishment of the Thirteenth CTC
Congress was to officially promulgate the principle of "to each
according to [his or her] work." This signified that the *fidelista*
incentive system would be replaced by a more balanced
mixture of moral and material incentives. Moral incentives
would still be used, but less extensively than in the late 1960s.

Material incentives would increase in importance, but they would be more carefully related to productivity, and the greater distributional inequality that they produced would be kept within strict bounds. As Chapter 7 discusses, revolutionary leaders later suggested that the incentive balance began to break down in 1980, when certain limits on the use of material incentives were lifted. But through the 1970s a rough balance seems to have been maintained.

After 1970, a variety of moral incentives continued to be used. First, beginning in 1971 many consumer goods, especially durables, were distributed so that their purchase depended much less on an individual's income. Refrigerators, TV sets, sewing machines, and other consumer durables were distributed to those workers with the greatest need and the best work records as judged by general workers' meetings or by union committees.[10]

Second, symbolic rewards continued to be granted for successful "socialist emulation." After 1973, individuals could be named "vanguard workers" if they exceeded work norms, conserved raw materials, observed work discipline, passed adult education courses, and participated in voluntary labor. In addition, work centers could be designated exemplary and given the honor of flying the Banner of the Heroes of Moncada.

Third, although voluntary labor tapered off in the sugar sector, its use continued elsewhere. To enable voluntary laborers to see the material benefits of their supposedly morally motivated efforts, after 1970 the resources realized on "red Sundays" and other voluntary work days were devoted to the construction of some highly visible facility for the whole society, such as a school or hospital.[11] Beginning in 1971, work centers volunteered to form "microbrigades" to construct housing and other facilities. Microbrigade volunteers received their regular pay, while the comrades left behind in the work center compensated for their absence with unpaid overtime, or "plus-work". This system flourished until 1980, when, for reasons that will be discussed in Chapter 7, it fell into disuse.

Material incentives were reemphasized after 1970 through the formal reintroduction of payment according to work norms. Bonuses of various sorts were granted for overfulfillment of norms, and wage cuts were instituted for underfulfillment. Overtime pay, which had been widely renounced in the late 1960s, was introduced; and, in 1980, a far-reaching general wage reform was promulgated.

This wage reform reduced present and possible future wages for a minority of the labor force. It formally outlawed historical and out-of-line wages, and it reduced the maximum wage for agricultural workers, as industrial development received greater emphasis. For the majority of the labor force, however, this reform increased wages. It increased the minimum wage for all categories of workers; it allowed bonuses to reach 15 to 25 percent of the actual wage; it pushed up the maximum wage for non-agricultural service and office workers, and for technical and managerial personnel; and it stretched the official wage scales for technicians and managers from twelve to twenty categories, matching the remuneration for these groups with levels of responsibility and educational preparation.

Although individuals without the requisite educational credentials could still be hired as technicians and managers, they had to be placed at their minimum wage level and could advance up the wage scale only as they obtained formal education. In these ways, the general wage reform favored the new professionals.[12]

To spark greater productive effort, opportunities for consumption were increased. In the first half of the 1970s, excess consumer liquidity was virtually eliminated, and the variety of consumer goods was increased. Although essential items would continue to be rationed, between 1970 and 1980 the types of products rationed fell from 94 to 21 percent of all types of consumer goods;[13] and a parallel market, offering goods at official but higher prices, was introduced.[14]

Beginning in 1980, the revolutionary leadership began to relax some of the restrictions on small-scale private enterprise that it had imposed in the Revolutionary Offensive of 1968. Private repair and other services were allowed and licensed. "Free" farmers' markets were opened, where farmers could sell a certain amount of their produce at whatever price the market would bear.[15] In 1984, a general law on housing was promulgated that, among other things, allowed individuals to construct, sell, and rent housing at free market prices.[16]

Material incentives were central to the new Economic Management and Planning System (*Sistema de Dirección y Planificación de la Economía*–SDPE), which Cuba adapted from Soviet practice at the time. The Cuban leadership began discussing the SDPE as early as 1973 and officially announced it in 1975. The SDPE's planning aspect was introduced immediately. The management part was gradually introduced later: Nine percent of Cuban enterprises were under SDPE by 1978, 55.8 percent by 1979, and 94.8 percent by 1980.[17]

As early as 1969, then-President Osvaldo Dorticós pointed out that multilevel and long-range planning and management, such as was entailed by the introduction of the SDPE, required a significant increase in the number of trained, new professional economic and managerial personnel.[18] These were needed to formulate, implement, adjust, and evaluate plans. At the same time, they were needed to manage day-to-day operations at all levels of the new economic system. In contrast to the *fidelista* system, which in the late 1960s had dumped both economic professionals and economic controls into "the garbage pail" (according to Dorticós),[19] the SDPE reintroduced economic controls and increased the demand for trained economic controllers.

The SDPE envisioned an elaborate planning process that would involve central planning authorities, sectoral and regional officials, and ministry, enterprise, and work center managers and workers.[20] No longer would Cuban planning be limited to annual or even shorter range plans. The Cubans introduced their first five-year plan in 1975 and their first twenty-year plan, which was to be updated every five years, in 1980.

This was the culmination of a process that had begun in 1972, when the Council for Mutual Economic Assistance (CMEA, the former Soviet bloc's common market) accepted Cuba as a full member. From then on, Cuban economic plans were coordinated with the plans of its CMEA partners. Cuba was to stabilize its deliveries of sugar to CMEA countries in return for various types of assistance.

Most notably, beginning in 1976 the price of Cuban sugar exports to the Soviet Union was indexed to the prices of Cuban imports from that country, especially petroleum. This was an extremely beneficial agreement at the time for the Cubans. But it was one of many factors that led them to continue relying heavily on sugar exports and to concentrate their trade with the Soviet bloc. By 1984, sugar still accounted for about three-quarters of the value of Cuba's exports, and the socialist countries accounted for over 86 percent of the value of Cuba's trade.

Under SDPE, the final plan was not supposed to determine the obligations of enterprises and work centers in detail. Instead, the plan was to determine key indicators, such as amount of physical output, average number of workers, amount of raw materials, and average level of productivity.

SDPE enterprises were supposed to be cost-accounting units, with profit (receipts minus costs at centrally fixed prices for materials, labor, and output) and profitability (the profit/capital ratio) serving as their main performance criteria. Exactly how these criteria would be met, however, was supposed to be largely left up to the enterprises themselves, which were envisioned as semiautonomous units.

SDPE enterprises were also supposed to have financial autonomy, with the right to maintain a bank account that no other organization could utilize. Enterprises could apply to the National Bank for loans, which they were supposed to pay back with interest in timely fashion. The National Bank was supposed to exercise financial control over SDPE enterprises, by denying further credit to those that failed in their payments. This, of course, was meant to encourage enterprises to operate efficiently.

In general, SDPE enterprises were supposed to realize a profit to maintain their credit rating, but also to accomplish a variety of other tasks. For example, SDPE enterprises were expected to pay a depreciation tax for the use of the basic means of production supplied to them by the state. They could also be held legally responsible for late deliveries, shoddy goods, failure to abide by contracts with other enterprises, and other malfeasance; and the fines that they could be required to pay were supposed to come from their profits.

Ultimately, SDPE enterprises were supposed to realize a profit in order to finance material incentive funds, an important motive force of the whole system. A sociocultural fund was to pay for such things as housing, day care centers, and dining halls for the enterprise labor force. Another fund was for rewarding enterprise personnel with personal and collective bonuses, in accordance with performance.[21] If the SDPE enterprise did not produce efficiently, did not realize a profit, did not meet its financial and other obligations, then it was not supposed to be allowed to set up and disburse these incentive funds—it was supposed to lose one of its main mechanisms of labor force motivation.

The introduction of the SDPE was supposed to make workers and managers materially responsible for their own economic performance and for that of their work center and enterprise. The idea was to make all workers and managers more conscious of the economy as a whole. And it was supposed to more closely integrate their individual interests with the collective interest of their enterprise and with the social interest of the whole economy. But the SDPE did not live up to these expectations. Its problems had many causes (see Chapter 6), but they stemmed in part from the behavior of the old cadres and the new professionals. By the mid-1980s, the revolutionary leadership was again revamping planning, management, and incentives.

Rectifying Political Organizations

The post-1970 rectification process set up democratic centralist forms of state administration that were adapted, with modifications, from Soviet practice at the time. These Organs of Popular Power (*Organos de Poder Popular*—OPP) were begun on an experimental basis in Matanzas province in 1974, approved by the First Party Congress in 1975, and codified in the new Cuban constitution in 1976. OPPs were extended across the island during 1976 and 1977. Although, as will be seen in Chapter 7, the OPPs recently have been reformed, they still retain much of their original structure.

The OPPs formally divide state responsibilities among national, provincial, and municipal offices overseen by bodies of elected representatives.[22] OPPs are empowered to oversee the production and service units that serve their areas. A municipal OPP, for example, might oversee local units such as schools, theaters, health facilities, factories, and restaurants. Neither municipal nor provincial OPPs, however, have unrestricted rein over the units assigned to them. They are not allowed, for example, to introduce their own schedule of prices, wages, school curricula, or statistical procedures. Such norms, procedures, and methods are controlled by central authorities, formally subordinated to the National Assembly of Popular Power.

The OPPs are charged with helping to overcome economic inefficiencies and to improve the delivery of goods and services to the population. To accomplish these ends, OPPs can appoint the management of the units under their jurisdiction and can impose a variety of sanctions if necessary. All OPP assemblies have a staff of trained personnel, whose expertise allows delegates to effectively carry out their oversight functions. The creation of OPPs thereby increased the demand for new professionals.

The OPPs are constituted from the neighborhood level upward.[23] After neighborhoods have nominated at least two candidates for each available seat in the municipal assembly, biographies of each candidate are circulated among the electors, the only form of "campaigning" that is allowed. Voters that make up a constituency then elect by secret ballot one of the candidates as their delegate to the municipal OPP. Until recently, the municipal delegates then elected the delegates to both the provincial and national OPP assemblies, from slates presented by nominating committees, composed of representatives of the mass and political organizations and chaired by a representative of the party.

The law required these committees in most instances to nominate at least 25 percent more candidates than available seats, and electors could reject the committees' slates in whole or in part. The law also required that a majority of the national delegates had to be elected first to the municipal level. Finally, again from slates presented by nominating committees, the municipal and provincial assemblies were empowered to elect their own executive committees, while the National Assembly would elect the Council of Ministers and the Council of State.

The National Assembly, according to the Cuban Constitution of 1976, is "the only organ in the Republic invested with constituent and legislative authority."[24] As such, the National Assembly is empowered to approve all laws, national economic plans, national budgets, and other nationwide legislation. When they created this assembly, however, Cuban revolutionaries did not jettison their customary practice of widely discussing drafts of fundamental laws and other important political documents with the population. According to the constitution, "when it is considered necessary in view of the nature of the law in question," the National Assembly may "submit it to the people for consultation."[25] Here, as in many other instances, the Cubans retained their more participatory practices as they adapted Soviet forms.

In fact, the OPP system provides a variety of mechanisms to encourage participation from the bottom up. OPP delegates at all levels, for example, are required to periodically report to their electors in formal "rendering of accounts" meetings. In these, delegates are obliged to report on their activities and on the pressing issues before their OPP, and electors are encouraged to raise their own issues. If the questions and concerns of the electors cannot be answered or resolved at the time, OPP delegates are required to present a satisfactory answer or resolution at the next regular meeting. In addition, the OPP system provides for the recall of delegates and the election of new ones at the pleasure of the majority of electors. Overall, the OPPs supply the population with a vehicle for attempting to solve problems, especially at the local level, and with a channel for voicing complaints, possibly up to the national level.

But ultimately the revolutionary leadership has dominated the OPPs by means of the nomination and election procedures, which (as Chapter 7 describes) have been reformed only recently. Through these procedures the revolutionary leadership has exercised considerable control over who could be nominated, and therefore, elected, to higher OPP posts. Not surprisingly, then, since the OPPs were introduced, an overwhelming majority of delegates to the higher assemblies have been members of the Communist Party or of the Union of Young Communists.[26]

It is through these that the revolutionary leadership has exercised control over the most important OPP decisions. As Raúl Castro explained:

> The party does not administer. ... The party can and must take suggestions, proposals, recommendations; it must counsel and guide the Organs of Popular Power, but must never hand down decisions, never impose decisions, never undertake any manner of reprisal as regards an Organ of Popular Power or members of such organs who do not agree with or will not carry out something the party has suggested, proposed, recommended, advised, or set down in a guideline. The party must use as its principal means to guarantee that its guidelines and criteria are put into practice by the Organs of Popular Power the work of the party members who are also delegates to those organs or members of their executive committee. Party members ... are obliged to comply with and carry out the decisions of the party and to convince ... the non-party members of the fairness of those decisions and the need to apply them. If, after exhausting all the methods and resources within their authority ... the party leadership at a given level ... does not convince the Organs of Popular

Power at that level to follow a recommendation or guideline that it considers important, it must then refer to the next highest level of the party ... to discuss the matter at ... [its] level of Popular Power.[27]

In other words, the party was not to directly administer the state or to command the decisions of non-party OPP delegates. But party members in OPP posts were to remain under party discipline and were obliged to attempt to persuade the OPP delegates to follow the party line. If this failed at the lower levels, then matters were to be taken to the next higher OPP level, where many more delegates would be party members, and where, as a consequence, conformity with the party line would ultimately be assured.

Raúl Castro's stricture against direct party administration reflects another aspect of the post-1970 rectification process. Unlike in the 1960s, the party after 1970 was officially defined as an organization limited to persuasion for setting its stamp on state and society.[28] In fact, the partial removal of the party from direct administration is what opened space for other organizations, including trade unions, economic units, and OPPs, to operate with some autonomy. Still, these organizations remain ultimately controlled by the revolutionary leadership.

This control is exercised not only through mechanisms analogous to those described by Raúl Castro for the OPP, but also directly through the "nomenclature," a list of posts that the party retains the exclusive right to fill with candidates of its choice.[29] There is no way to know how many of these posts are intermediate-level or who these candidates are. But given the leadership's post-1970 policy of favoring new professionals over old cadres, the intermediate posts involved have doubtless commonly gone to new professionals.

Rectifying the Educational System

To address decisively the shortage of skills and to increase the supply of new professionals, the Cubans began to focus on reforming their educational system in the 1970 to 1971 school year. Then, teachers in every school and cultural workers in every province met to "analyze and debate the principal problems of education," as the Ministry of Education reported later.[30] These meetings gave rise to Cuba's First National Congress of Education and Culture, held in Havana in April 1971. This congress directed the Ministry of Education to undertake a diagnostic study of Cuban education at all levels. This study, begun in the 1972 to 1973 school year, resulted in the Plan for Improving and Developing the National Educational System (*El plan de perfeccionamiento y desarrollo del Sistema Nacional de Educación de Cuba*), which was approved by the First Congress of the Cuban Communist Party and the Ministry of Education in 1975.[31]

As a result of this renewed attention, the educational system began to expand more rapidly and surely than in the 1960s. Enrollments in the adult education system expanded consistently from 316,896 from 1970 to 1971 to 701,259 from 1976 to 1977 (see Table 4.1 in appendix). The tapering off of these enrollments between the school year from 1977 to 1978 and from 1980 to 1981 was probably due to success rather than failure. Adult illiteracy had reportedly been reduced by 1980 to 4.0 percent, and by 1981 to 1.9 percent of Cubans between twenty and forty-nine years old that were "able to study."[32] In 1980, the government declared victory in the "Battle for the Sixth Grade" and in the struggle for the ninth grade by 1985.[33]

Primary school enrollments rose to a high of 1,801,191 from 1974 to 1975 and then gradually declined (see Table 4.1). By the school year from 1983 to 1984, there were almost a quarter million fewer students enrolled at the primary level than from 1970 to 1971, and a 28.8 percent drop from the peak year from 1974 to 1975. The steady drop in primary level enrollments in the second half of the 1970s and early 1980s was due to both demographic change and improved efficiency.

On the one hand, primary-level enrollment dropped as the birth rate slowed. The birth rate, which was 26.1 per thousand in 1958, soared to 35.1 per thousand by 1963 with the initial revolutionary improvements in living conditions and health care, but then began a steady decline to 15.8 per thousand by 1979.[34] It is clear that this declining birth rate explains the decline in primary school enrollments and not a falling-off of enrollment efforts, because, between the 1974 to 1975 year and the 1980 to 1981 year, the percentage of the six- to twelve-year-old age group attending school rose from 98.4 to 98.8 percent.[35]

Declining primary school enrollments also resulted from improved efficiency. As mentioned earlier, of the class that entered first grade in 1964 and was scheduled to complete sixth grade in 1970, only 20.7 percent were graduated on time.[36] In 1981, however, reportedly due to various curricular changes and improved teacher training, 70.8 percent of the primary-level students who had begun in 1975 were successfully graduated.[37]

Although both adult and primary education recovered from some of their problems of the late 1960s and scored new successes after 1970, it was in secondary and higher education that enrollments expanded most dramatically. As primary-level enrollments dropped from 83.3 percent of total enrollments in the 1970 to 1971 year to 48.5 percent from 1983 to 1984, secondary enrollments went from 14.8 to 43.1 percent, and higher education from 1.9 to 8.4 percent (see Table 4.2 in appendix).

In part, the astounding expansion of secondary education after 1970 was made possible by improvements at the primary level, which was readying greater numbers of students to enter secondary grades, just as the expansion of higher education resulted from improvements at the secondary level. In addition, the emphasis put on higher education in this period allowed many more to undertake university training at a younger age. This new emphasis was symbolized perhaps most clearly by the creation in 1977 of a separate Ministry of Higher Education.[38]

But the change in the structure of total enrollments was also the result of the post-1970 rectification of major economic and political organizations that increased the demand for trained personnel—the new professionals—to enter intermediate-level occupations. In the 1970s, the policy of coopting individuals into these occupations primarily on the basis of political credentials was stopped. The minimum qualification for entry into these occupations became a secondary degree. Thus, supplying sufficient numbers of new professionals required expanding secondary and higher education far beyond what had been done in the 1960s.

Enrollments in secondary education rose steadily from 272,193 in the 1970 to 1971 year to a high of 1,182,600 from 1981 to 1982, dipped by almost 66,000 in the 1982 to 1983 year and then rose again from 1983 to 1984 (see Table 4.1). In the 1970 to 1971 year, only 63.8 percent of the thirteen- to sixteen-year-old group was in school, while from 1981 to 1982 this figure had risen to 84.0 percent.[39] Since secondary education still required expansion in the early 1980s, the reason for the drop in enrollment from 1982 to 1983 is unclear. In any event, the general trend was for secondary education enrollments to expand dramatically after 1970.

From the limited data available, it would seem that, as the

secondary system expanded, it also became more efficient. Retention rates, the ratio between the number of students enrolled at the beginning and at the end of an academic year, increased for all types of secondary schools for which data are available (see Table 4.3 in appendix). Between the 1970 to 1971 and the 1982 to 1983 school years, the retention rate for basic secondary school (grades 7 to 9) increased from 84.1 percent to 94.2 percent; for preuniversities (grades 10 to 12), from 86.5 percent to 93.2 percent; and for teacher training schools (grades 10 to 13), from 72.8 percent to 92.5 percent.

Since the figures are obtained by dividing the number of students at the beginning of the year by the number of students at the end of the year, it should be noted that retention bears no necessary relationship to the number of students who passed an academic year, for it includes those still enrolled at the end of the year whether they passed or failed. Retention rates also give only a rough idea of how many students dropped out during the school year, for these would be partly compensated for by others who entered school late in the academic year. But even with these limitations, the improved retention rates suggest that the efficiency of Cuba's secondary education system increased substantially after 1970.

Some of the more dramatic changes in Cuban education after 1970 took place in higher education. In the 1974 to 1975 year the country still had only five higher education centers, but by 1984 to 1985 it had forty-six.[40] Enrollment at this level expanded from 35,137 during 1970 to 1971, to 205,000 in the 1980 to 1981 year, stagnated for a couple of years, and then reached 240,000 in the 1984 to 1985 year (see Table 4.1). Between 1970 to 1971 and 1984 to 1985, higher education enrollments increased by a remarkable 583 percent.

After 1970, the Cubans also began to develop a system of graduate education in their major university centers. During the 1960s, revolutionary Cuba did not offer graduate degrees but only graduate courses taught by foreign experts and designed to improve the higher education teaching staff. By 1971, however, a system for granting advanced degrees at the masters and doctoral levels was being developed, and in 1972 a Commission for the Study of Scientific Grades was set up to determine the objectives and requirements for advanced degrees for professors, researchers, and new professionals in production and services.[41] Ten years later, in 1982 to 1983, almost 19,000 students attended 994 graduate courses.[42]

Not only did higher education enrollments expand after 1970, their distribution by subject area changed considerably (see Table 4.4 in appendix). As the post-1970 development strategy placed less stress on agricultural and more on industrial expansion, technology enrollments outpaced those in agricultural sciences. Enrollments in education, economic studies, humanities, social sciences, and art, which had all declined in absolute as well as relative numbers in the 1960s, expanded the most in the 1970s. A dramatic 4,725.6 percent increase in education enrollments signified the emphasis put on improving teachers' qualifications. An impressive 1,665.2 percent increase in economic studies enrollments went hand in hand with the replacement of the *fidelista* system by organizational structures that increased the demand for economic professionals after 1970.

In order to meet this increased demand, after 1970 education in economic studies was revamped. In 1970, a new Institute of Economy was created at Camagüey to complement those that had already existed in the 1960s at Santiago, Santa Clara, and Havana.[43] In 1973 the Vice-Ministry of Higher Education (forerunner to the Ministry) sought to overcome the results of the *fidelista* denigration of economic studies in the 1960s by creating a unified national curriculum for training economics professionals. Study toward the degree of Licentiate in Political Economy was begun in 1974, to train future professors for the new curriculum.[44]

In June 1970, the Institute of Economy at the University of Havana initiated its first graduate courses, aimed at upgrading and expanding the skills and knowledge of those who had been trained in the 1960s. In August 1973, the first masters degrees were granted to students in regional economic planning.[45] Beginning in the 1973 to 1974 year, it became possible for those pursuing economics studies in Cuba to prepare for a doctoral degree (*Candidato a Doctor en Ciéncias Económicas*) that would be granted by Moscow State University.[46] By 1982, seventeen Cuban professors of economics had successfully completed this degree.[47]

A National School for Economic Management (*Escuela Nacional de Dirección de la Economía*—ENDE) was opened in 1976, specifically to train economic professionals in the workings of the new SDPE.[48] After the first semester of ENDE's existence, it became clear that diffusing this knowledge to all who needed it was too much for this one school. Beginning in July 1976, offshoots of ENDE were set up across the country, and by 1980 each province had such a school. Between 1976 and 1980, this network of schools trained 5,608 enterprise managers, 3,567 assistant economic managers, 627 state and organizational managers, and 290 professors. In 1978, ENDE became the Higher Institute of Economic Management. In 1985, this institute graduated its first cohort of Licentiates in Economic Management.

Educational expansion and improvement, then, increased Cuba's supply of economic and other new professionals needed to operate the new organizational setup. As Chapter 6 explains, Cuba's post-1970 system often performed in a bureaucratic centralist fashion. But the new system and the Soviet-inspired democratic centralist principles upon which it was based called forth the dramatic rise of the new professionals.

Notes

1. I characterize the post-1970 period as one of "rectification" rather than one of "institutionalization," the overly narrow term commonly used by Cubans and Cuba scholars. The new organizations and procedures represented only one aspect of the changes introduced in this period, which also included the change in development strategy and the dramatic expansion and transformation of education after 1970.
2. Gonzalo M. Rodríguez Mesa, "El desarrollo industrial de Cuba y la maduración de inversiones," *Economía y Desarrollo* 68 (May/June 1982): 127.
3. For the fullest statement of the "Sovietization thesis" so far, see Carmelo Mesa-Lago, *Cuba in the 1970s* (Albuquerque: University of New Mexico Press, 1974). For a full critique of this and other formulations of the thesis, see Frank T. Fitzgerald, "A Critique of the 'Sovietization of Cuba' Thesis," *Science & Society* 42, no. 1 (Spring 1978): 1-32; and Frank T. Fitzgerald, "The 'Sovietization of Cuba Thesis' Revisited," simultaneously published in Andrew Zimbalist, ed., *Cuban Political Economy: Controversies in Cubanology* (Boulder, CO: Westview Press, 1988), pp. 137-53, and in *Science & Society* 51, no. 4 (Winter 1987-1988): 439-57.
4. Max Weber, "Bureaucracy," in Hans Gerth and C. Wright Mills (eds.), *From Max Weber: Essays in Sociology* (New York: Oxford University Press, 1958), pp. 196-244.
5. This term "democratic centralism" stems, of course, from Lenin's writings and their subsequent interpretation in Soviet Marxism. For representative Cuban descriptions of the "democratic centralist" process, see Orlando Carnota, "La profesión de administrador," *Economía y Desarrollo* 23 (May/June 1974): 47-67; and Ovidio D'Angelo Hernández, "Algunos aspectos sociales de la gestión de empresas," *Economía y Desarrollo* 44 (November/December 1977): 30-45.

6. *Granma Weekly Review,* 7 May 1972.
7. Alfredo Suarez, General Secretary, Transport Workers Union, as quoted in Marifeli Pérez-Stable, "Whither the Cuban Working Class?" *Latin American Perspectives,* Supplement 1975, p. 70.
8. Linda Fuller, "Politics of Worker's Control in Cuba, 1959-1982: The Work Center and the National Arena" (Ph.D. diss., University of California, Berkeley, 1985), pp. 423-425; also see her *Work and Democracy in Socialist Cuba* (Philadelphia: Temple University Press, 1992).
9. *Memorias del XIII Congreso de la CTC* (Havana: 1973), pp. 15, 181.
10. See Arthur MacEwan, "Incentives, Equality, and Power in Revolutionary Cuba," in Ronald Radosh, ed., *The New Cuba* (New York: Morrow, 1976), p. 89.
11. Author's interview HGO1.80.
12. For these new scales, see Claes Brundenius, *Economic Growth, Basic Needs and Income Distribution in Revolutionary Cuba* (Lund, Sweden: University of Lund, 1981), p. 153; for an explanation of this reform and its official rationale, see "General Wage Reform," *Granma Weekly Review,* 6 April 1980, pp. 4-5; and Joaquín Benavides Rodríguez, "La ley de la distribución con arreglo al trabajo y la reforma de salarios en Cuba," *Cuba Socialista* 2 (March 1982): 62-93. For the bonus percentages, see Marifeli Pérez-Stable, "Politics and *Conciencia* in Revolutionary Cuba, 1959-1984" (Ph.D. diss., State University of New York at Stony Brook, 1985), p. 200.
13. Author's computation based on data supplied by Eugenio Balari, Director of the Cuban Institute of Internal Demand.
14. For a detailed discussion of the parallel market and its rationale, see Humberto Pérez, *Sobre las dificultades objectivas de la revolución: lo que el pueblo debe saber* (Havana: Editorial Política, 1979), pp. 82-92.
15. For useful information on these changes, see "Cuba's New 'Free Market,'" *Cuba Update* 1, no. 3 (September 1980): 1-2; Medea Benjamin, et al., *No Free Lunch: Food and Revolution in Cuba Today* (San Francisco: Institute for Food and Development Policy, 1984), chap. 5; Jonathan Rosenberg, "Cuba's Free Market

Experiment," *Latin American Research Review* 27, no. 3 (1992): 51–89.

16. For the text of this law, see *Revista Cubana de Derecho* 24 (1985): 37–78.

17. Justa Hernández Hernández and Vasili Nikolenkov, "El mechanismo económico del socialismo," *Economía y Desarrollo* 68 (September/October 1985): 77. For Cuban descriptions of the SDPE, see "Sobre el sistema de dirección y planifición de la economía," in Primer Congreso del Partido Comunista de Cuba, *Tesis y Resoluciones* (Havana: Editorial de Ciencias Sociales, 1979); and Raúl Martel, *La empresa socialista* (Editorial de Ciencias Sociales, 1979).

18. Osvaldo Dorticós, *Discurso en el acto de presentación de los militantes del partido del Instituto de Economía* (Havana: Editorial de Ciencias Sociales, 1969).

19. Osvaldo Dorticós, "Control económico y normación: tareas del primer orden," *Economía y Desarrollo* 11 (May/June 1972): 34.

20. For a vivid description of the planning process at the work center level, see Marta Harnecker, *Cuba: Democracy or Dictatorship?* (Westport, CT: Lawrence Hill, 1980), chap. 1.

21. SDPE initially envisioned a third incentive fund to finance microinvestments by the enterprise, but this apparently was never instituted in Cuba.

22. The details on the formal structure of the OPP are taken from the *Constitution of the Republic of Cuba* (New York: Center for Cuban Studies, 1976), chaps. 7–9; and *Reglamento de las Asambleas Nacional, Provincial, y Municipal del Poder Popular* (Havana: Editorial Obre, 1979).

23. For a brief discussion of the Cuban electoral and nominating system in this period, see René González Mendoza, "The Electoral System in Cuba," *Granma Weekly Review*, 21 December 1986, p. 2.

24. *Cuban Constitution*, Chap. 7, Art. 68.

25. Ibid., Chap. 7, Art. 73.

26. See Cynthia Cockburn, "People's Power," in John Griffiths and Peter Griffiths (eds.), *Cuba: The Second Decade* (London: Writers and Readers Publishing Cooperative, 1979), pp. 18–35; and Archibald R.M. Ritter, "The Organs of People's Power and the

Communist Party: The Nature of Cuban Democracy," in Sandor Halebsky and John M. Kirk (eds.), *Cuba: Twenty-Five Years of Revolution* (New York: Praeger, 1985), pp. 270-90.

27. In Michael Taber (ed.), *Fidel Castro Speeches, Vol. 2: Our Power is That of the Working People* (New York: Pathfinder Press, 1983), pp. 234-35.

28. Since 1970, the party has undergone a series of other changes as well. Perhaps most important, it has regularly held congresses, developed an explicit program, and expanded its membership considerably.

29. "Sobre la política de formación, selección, ubicación, promoción y superación de los cuadros," in Primer Congreso, *Tesis y Resoluciones,* pp. 57-99.

30. Ministro de Educación, *El plan de perfeccionamiento y desarrollo del Sistema Nacional de Educación de Cuba* (Havana: 1976), p. 11.

31. Ministerio de Educación, *El plan de perfeccionamiento,* "Introducción"; and Primer Congreso, *Tesis y Resoluciones,* pp. 363-422.

32. The 1980 figure was reported by Brundenius, *Economic Growth,* p. 125; the 1981 figure is from *Granma Weekly Review,* 29 January 1984, p. 4.

33. Fidel Castro, "Main Report to the Third Congress of the Communist Party of Cuba," *Granma Weekly Review,* Feb. 16, 1986, p. 5.

34. Sergio Díaz-Briquets and Lisandro Pérez, *Cuba: The Demography of Revolution* (Washington, DC: Population Reference Bureau, 1981), pp. 12-13.

35. For 1974 to 1975, Ministerio de Educación, *Informe a la Asamblea Nacional del Poder Popular* (Havana: 1981), p. 372; for 1980 to 1981, *Granma Weekly Review,* 29 January 1984, p. 4.

36. Ministerio de Educación, *El plan de prefeccionamiento,* p. 63.

37. Nikolai Kolesnikov, *Cuba: educación popular y preparación de los cuadros nacionales, 1959-1982* (Moscow: Editorial Progreso, 1983). p. 287; "Interview with José R. Fernández, Minister of Education," and "Teaching Staff Improvements," *Cuba Update* 1, no. 6 (January 1981): 3 and 12, respectively.

38. "Ley que crea el Ministerio de Educación Superior," *Universidad de la Habana*, Nos. 203-204 (1976), pp. 171-75.

39. For 1970 to 1971, Ministerio de Educación, *Informe*, p. 372; for 1981 to 1982, Kolesnikov, *Cuba*, p.285.

40. For 1974 to 1975, Concepción Duchesne, "Incremento y desarrollo en la educación superior, 1976-1980," *Bohemia*, 28 November 1980, p. 36; for 1984 to 1985, Fidel Castro, "Main Report to the Third Congress," p. 5.

41. *Economía y Desarrollo* 14 (November/December 1972): 212.

42. Kolesnikov, *Cuba*, p. 422. For further details on the Cuban system of graduate education, see Emilio Fernández Conde, "La educación postgraduada," *Sobre Educación Superior*, July/December 1971, pp. 77-92; the summary of the report of the Cuban delegation to the Sixth Conference of Ministers of Higher Education of the Socialist Countries, in Bucharest, October 1971, in *Economía y Desarrollo* 9 (January/February 1972), esp. pp. 212-14; Oscar F. Rego, "Los cursos de postgrado especializados," *Bohemia*, 30 November 1979; and Concepción Duchesne, "Superación profesional," *Bohemia*, 23 January 1981.

43. "Académicas," *Economía y Desarrollo* 13 (September/October 1972): 225.

44. Alexis Codina Jiménez and Joaquín Fernández, "Apuntos en el XX aniversario del inicio de la formación de economistas," *Economía y Desarrollo* 71 (November/December 1982): 23-25.

45. *Economía y Desarrollo* 18 (July/August 1973): 210.

46. "Académicas," *Economía y Desarrollo* 23 (May-June 1974).

47. Codina Jiménez and Fernández, "Apuntos en el XX aniversario," p. 32.

48. Rosendo Morales, "La preparación de los cuadros dirigentes de la economía del país," *Cuba Socialista* 4 (November/December 1982): 108-33.

Chapter 5

Managing the Transition from Old Cadres to New Professionals

In the post-1970 rectification process, with its transition from old (political) cadres to new professionals, some lost, some gained, and some had to transform themselves as the situation demanded. Everyone had to adjust.

The revolutionary leadership, as a consequence, had to handle this transition with care. It had to discourage old cadres from resisting this transition, and encourage them to turn themselves into new professionals through education. It had to share some decision making with new professionals, and define the limits of their decision-making power. Lastly, it had to ensure the new professionals' commitment to revolutionary goals.

This chapter will examine the attempts of the Cuban revolutionary government to respond to these challenges. Other questions that appeared and became urgent as the process developed will also be considered. These include: the class background of the majority of new professionals; the proportion of women among the new professionals; and how the revolutionary leadership tried to shape the political consciousness of the new professionals.

Criticizing and Reassuring the Old Cadres

Cuba's old cadres were criticized early for lacking the requisite know-how and formal education to perform their work well. Fidel Castro pointed to their administrative inadequacies in explaining the failure to reach the 10-million-ton sugar harvest goal in 1970. After that, other leaders and new professionals frequently lodged such public complaints.

The basis of such complaints was shown by the level of some of the how-to guides for administrators, written for old cadres by new professionals in the early 1970s. Among other things, these typically contained very elementary guidelines—for using personal calendars, preparing reports and memos, using work plans, evaluating subordinates, holding meetings, and so on. The following outline for carrying out a meeting was characteristic of this genre:

(1) Be sure the meeting is necessary.
(2) Invite only those who can add something to the discussion.
(3) Use meetings only for collective discussion, not for disseminating information.
(4) Hold the meeting in an orderly fashion.
(5) Pay attention to what is said.
(6) Keep the discussion on the topic.
(7) Learn to discover when the topic is exhausted.
(8) End the discussion with a concrete conclusion.[1]

This list clearly illustrates that many old cadres were perceived as lacking even the most basic administrative sense.

Also in the early 1970s, some old cadres were criticized for being "chatterers." To cover up their ignorance or their inability to organize themselves and others to accomplish goals, this breed of old cadres were constantly incanting "Patria o Muerte!" and similar revolutionary slogans.[2] They spent their workday pretending to be busy by holding endless meetings, which were social gatherings rather than working sessions. Whether their chatter was revolutionary or social, they accomplished little and they prevented others from accomplishing much.[3]

In the same period, other old cadres sometimes were dubbed "super-executives." Unwilling or unable to delegate responsibility to subordinates, they tried to oversee everything themselves. Without plan, they scurried from place to place, hopped out of their jeep to check others' work, issued some orders, and then roared off again. Old cadre super-executives thrived on impressing others with their initiative, audacity, decisiveness, and dynamism, regardless of their concrete accomplishments, which were few.[4]

Both types of behavior can be seen as part of the legacy of the *fidelista* system of the late 1960s. Many chatterers and super-executives could be expected among cadres with little know-how, who were confronted with very ambitious goals and forced out of their offices and into factories and fields by the antibureaucratic struggle. Many probably had little choice but to chatter or dash about. Criticisms of chatterers and super-executives were widely expressed only in the first half of the 1970s, indicating perhaps that these holdovers from the *fidelista* period began to disappear relatively soon.

Another aspect of the *fidelista* legacy, however, appears to have endured longer. In the late 1960s, it will be remembered, mass participation in decision-making atrophied. The people lacked institutionalized means for making suggestions and registering complaints; they were expected to simply follow orders. Through this experience, many old cadres developed the habit of avoiding popular participation, and this seems to have lived on. As late as 1979, Humberto Pérez, the head of the Central Planning Board (JUCEPLAN) at that time, could still complain of "*compañeros* who work in the distinct state organizations, including ... Popular Power" who were "im-

pregnated with the old centralizing and in many cases bureaucratic habits."[5] Some old cadres who remained in intermediate
occupations after 1970 might have overcome their bureaucratic
habits, but many others had not.[6] As the next chapter explains,
the latter were one force blocking the full implementation of
democratic centralist principles in the late 1970s and early
1980s.

After 1970, Cuba's old cadres were destined to be turned into
or replaced by new professionals. But while many old cadres
found transforming themselves into new professionals
through education beyond their ability or inclination, they
tried to resist being displaced. Such old cadres developed
self-protective strategies for retaining intermediate positions
despite their relative lack of formal training. Raúl Castro spoke
of them in October 1979 when he complained of individuals
who "are more concerned about retaining the positions they
hold than about the needs of the people they are supposed to
serve."[7] He went on to explain that such administrative personnel typically engaged in "buddyism"—that is, they colluded
with coworkers in covering up poor work performance and
other failings to protect their positions.[8]

The buddyism referred to by Raúl Castro was not a form of
self-protectiveness solely for old cadres; new professionals
could also sometimes engage in this behavior. But, given that
old cadre positions were threatened in ways that new professional positions were not, the incidence and intensity of
buddyism among old cadres was probably much greater.

In 1975 the revolutionary leadership promulgated a policy
for training, selecting, evaluating, and promoting members of
the administrative apparatus.[9] This policy was designed partly
to reassure the old cadres and to reduce their resistance. At the
same time, it favored the new professionals by stipulating that
intermediate-level positions should go to those with the appro-

priate formal educational preparation. According to the policy, everyone should be periodically and systematically evaluated, and these evaluations should be objective rather than arbitrary in order to prevent the development of "insecurity among the cadres."[10]

Objective evaluation could be achieved in two ways. First, it required that personal traits not be the main focus except as they affected work performance, that everyone be allowed to appeal their evaluation, and that a wide range of people be consulted about each individual. Not only was the individual's immediate supervisor to be involved, but coworkers, subordinates, trade union and party officials, and others as well. Second, objective evaluations required that both positive and negative aspects of each individual's work performance be examined. Evaluations were to respect the old cadres' experience, and they were not to discourage but to spur individuals to do better.

Thus, the old cadres were encouraged to take up formal study, which, in part, explains the continuing viability of the adult education system, discussed earlier. The leadership saw this as a means for the old cadres to convert themselves into new professionals.

In fact, the requirement that intermediate-level positions be awarded on the basis of educational preparation was applied most consistently in the more exacting specialties—such as medicine, law, architecture, biotechnology, etc.—and in the more exacting positions—such as those of top executives, technicians, scientists, university professors, etc. Without question, even minimal job performance in these professions required specialized, technical, or extensive knowledge, and not surprisingly they were the most likely to be filled with new professionals.

But, as noted below, the old cadres hung on in all but the

very top management positions and in older sectors of the economy that had been permeated by the *fidelista* notion: that economic management required nothing more than political loyalty and work experience. In these areas, old cadre administrators long continued to hire and promote their old cadre "buddies" over new professional competitors.[11] As late as 1988, Fidel Castro found it necessary to reiterate that intermediate-level positions should be awarded on the basis of educational credentials, not seniority, a mainstay of the old cadres.[12]

Thus, the revolutionary leadership favored the new professionals and criticized the old cadres for incompetence, poor work-styles, buddyism, and promotion by seniority. Still, the leadership recognized that it could not dispense with the old cadres overnight. Until the supply of new professionals was sufficiently large, after all, old cadres would likely have been replaced by others with similar educational deficits and perhaps even less experience.

So the leadership opted, not for a rapid purge, but for a gradual transition. A policy was undertaken that sought to increase the possibilities for old cadres to convert themselves into new professionals and to minimize resistance by old cadres who feared displacement by new professionals. But the best laid plans could not stop resistance from arising in those areas where large numbers of old cadres hung on.

The Pace of the Transition

Whatever resistance the old cadres mustered, however, the transition to new professionals was destined to proceed. The overall pace of this transition can be seen partly in Cuba's growing number of secondary school graduates. Between the school year 1959 to 1960 and 1979 to 1980, 510,957 Cuban students attained the secondary degree that would allow them to enter intermediate-level occupations as new professionals (see Table 5.1 in appendix). About 83 percent of the professionals educated in Cuba between 1959 and 1980 received their secondary school degrees after 1971, and about 52 percent after 1977. The creation of new professionals in Cuba first took off in the 1970s, and accelerated dramatically as the decade proceeded.

But when did the number of secondary school graduates catch up to the drain of professionals from Cuba? Estimating this requires adjusting for the number of intermediate-level personnel trained before the revolution, most of whom, as noted in Chapter 2, stayed on the island. In 1959, Cuba had an estimated 117,375 secondary school graduates (see Table 5.2 in appendix). This number dropped to a low of 103,439 by 1962 and did not recover its 1959 level until the period from 1969 to 1971, at the end of which an estimated 121,080 secondary school graduates remained in Cuba. The secondary education expansion did not begin to compensate fully for the exodus drain until the end of the revolution's first decade. During the 1970s, however, the number of secondary school graduates far outstripped the drain created by the exodus. By 1980, there were an estimated 532,980 secondary school graduates in Cuba, over 4.5 times as many as in 1959.[13]

This estimate of 532,980 secondary school graduates by 1980 can be combined with other data to arrive at three other estimates: First, by dividing 532,980 into 147,150, the number of Cuban professionals with higher education degrees, it is estimated that roughly 28 percent of Cuban professionals held higher education degrees by 1980.[14]

Second, some proportion of the 532,980 secondary school graduates in 1980 were pursuing their higher education full time, and were not actually in the labor force. If it is assumed that these numbered 100,000, or slightly less than half of the total number of students—the rest being either part-time or correspondence students—enrolled in higher education in the 1979 to 1980 year (see Table 4.1), then an estimated 432,980 new professionals were actually in the Cuban labor force in 1980.

Third, this figure of 432,980 new professional labor force participants in 1980 can be subtracted from 844,300,[15] the total number of Cubans in intermediate-level occupations in 1979, to estimate the number of old cadres at about 411,320. According to this, by 1980 the old cadres held on to about 49 percent of Cuba's intermediate-level positions. This reflected to some extent both the policy of gradual transition from old cadres to new professionals and the old cadres' ability to resist displacement by new professionals. Still, by 1980 the number of old cadres had just been surpassed by the number of new professionals, who had by then taken over an estimated 51 percent of Cuba's intermediate-level posts.

This, of course, was the overall trend and not the pattern in every particular area. As pointed out above, new professionals moved first into those intermediate occupations that everyone agreed required highly specialized, technical, or extensive knowledge. Old cadres, on the other hand, remained in many intermediate positions, especially managerial positions in older areas of the economy. Even as late as 1988, a Cuban study found that only 18 percent of the country's economic mangers held university degrees, 40 percent lacked the requisite education for their positions, and 34 percent possessed a ninth grade education or less.[16] According to another Cuban study, the situation was even worse in Villa Clara province: there, in 1988, the proportion of managers with a ninth grade education or less reached 44 percent.[17] Since new professionals require at least a twelfth grade education, as recently as 1988, the majority of Villa Clara's managers still may have been old cadres.

The New Professionals' Class Background and Gender Composition

From what class backgrounds have the new professionals come? Unfortunately, the data are not available to answer this question with assurance. But if the little information that has been published is manipulated with ingenuity, two interesting hypotheses can be suggested.

The only available data concerns the educational levels of parents of entrants to a single Cuban institution of higher education for one particular year (see Table 5.3 in appendix). Almost half of the new entrants to the University of Havana in the 1970 to 1971 year had fathers with only some primary schooling, and 60 percent had mothers with only such education. Furthermore, 19 percent had fathers and 17 percent had mothers with only some basic secondary training, while 14 percent had fathers and 12 percent mothers with some advanced secondary education, and only 10 percent had fathers and 5 percent mothers with at least some higher education. The fact that the parents of up to three-quarters of new entrants to the University of Havana in that year had no more than a basic secondary education suggests a dramatic redistribution of educational opportunities in the first decade of the revolution.

Assuming that these data were characteristic of all Cuban higher education students in that year, the chance of potential fathers, males aged fifteen to forty-four in 1953, to generate a child in higher education in 1970 to 1971 can be estimated (see Table 5.4 in appendix). Potential fathers as a whole had a 2.63 chance out of 100 to have such a child, while potential fathers with only primary education had less than two chances out of 100 to have such a child, and potential fathers with no formal education may have had less than one chance in 100.[18]

By contrast, potential fathers with basic secondary and

medium secondary educations had seventeen and twenty chances out of 100, respectively, while those with higher education backgrounds had only thirteen chances out of 100. The rather substantial drop that takes place in these data when moving from the advanced secondary to the higher education background is most likely due to the fact that potential fathers with higher education were more likely to join the early exodus from revolutionary Cuba, taking their university-bound children with them.

Unfortunately, given the limits of the available data about the redistribution of educational chances, it is possible to suggest only hypotheses, and only about the period up to the early 1970s. After the revolution's first decade, children from prerevolutionary intermediate- and higher-level educational backgrounds still retained a relative advantage over those from lower-level backgrounds in their ability to enter higher education and to become new professionals—but lost their absolute advantage. By the opening of the 1970 to 1971 academic year, the majority of new professionals were originating from the upper levels of the poorer, less educated stratum of Cuban society.

Fortunately, better data are available on the distribution of new professionals by gender. By 1980, women made up 31.4 percent of the Cuban labor force.[19] Their representation among new professionals, however, was considerably higher (see Table 5.5 in appendix): Women comprised 42.7 percent of all Cubans who had been graduated as medium-level technicians, at the lower level of the new professional category, and 40.1 percent of all those who had received higher education degrees.

Furthermore, women had become the majority among Cuba's youngest and therefore generally most recent graduates: They made up 52.2 percent of all seventeen- to nineteen-

year-olds who had been graduated as medium-level technicians and 54.3 percent of all twenty- to twenty-four-year-olds
with higher education degrees. If this trend continued, women
would eventually comprise the majority of all new professionals.

Equally striking, Cuba's new professional women were
increasingly receiving degrees in fields traditionally dominated
by men. Prior to the revolution, only a handful of Cuban
women pursued scientific or technical degrees.[20] By 1980,
however, significant numbers of women had moved into these
areas (see Table 5.5): Women already comprised a majority of
Cuba's higher education graduates in the natural and exact
sciences, and women made up the majority of Cuba's youngest,
generally most recent higher education graduates in geology,
mining, and metallurgy; sugar, chemical, and food industries;
agriculture and livestock; and economic studies. Only in education, where women had long predominated at the primary
and secondary levels, was there a decline in the percentage of
young women entrants.

Cuban women were making headway not just at the lower
and middle reaches of the professions. By the 1984 to 1985
academic year, for example, women made up 40 percent both
of academic administrators and of teachers in higher education.

At the same time, women held almost a quarter of Cuba's
doctoral degrees (*Candidato a Doctor*, equivalent to the Ph.D.).
They held 20.7 percent of such degrees in the biomedical
sciences, 24 percent in the agricultural sciences, 25.6 percent
in the natural sciences, 43.6 percent in education, and 48.1
percent in the humanities and social sciences. Women held
much smaller shares of doctoral degrees in the technical and
in the economic sciences—respectively, 9.1 and 17.4 percent—
but these shares were destined to grow, because numerous
younger women had begun to study these topics.[21]

By the 1980s, then, women comprised a sizeable and growing proportion of Cuba's new professionals. Still, the new professional women had not yet achieved parity with their male counterparts. The reasons for this were many. But one important reason (which is explored in Chapter 7) was the continuation of traditional discrimination against women in general, and against new professional women in particular.

Delimiting and Shaping the New Professionals

The role of the new professionals in Cuban society expanded dramatically after 1970. New professionals increasingly exercised the everyday decision-making power of intermediate-level posts. But they also increasingly helped to formulate, evaluate, and implement higher-level policy. Among many other things, new professionals were regularly conducting research in nationally prioritized areas, such as biotechnology; evaluating state investment projects; testing various incentive schemes; and sitting, as needed, on national study groups examining legal, political, social, psychological, economic, and other types of issues. By taking note of the findings of such research in its policy discussions and pronouncements, the Cuban leadership has increasingly confirmed the growing importance of the new professionals.[22]

But there has also been an attempt to delimit the new professionals' spheres of responsibility and decision making in relation to the leadership. The principles of democratic centralism called for this, of course, but only theoretically and very generally. To see how the new professional role was defined practically and specifically, one must look at the development of economic professionals in the post-1970 period.

As they increased in number, Cuba's economic professionals were outfitted with various media of professional communication. *Economía y Desarrollo*, the first journal of the profession, for example, appeared in early 1970. Although it regularly carried articles by Soviet-bloc authors, in its first twelve years of existence, *Economía y Desarrollo* published 472 articles, 72 percent of which were written by Cubans.[23] In 1978, the Central Planning Board (JUCEPLAN) started publishing *Cuestiones de la Economía*, which carried articles relevant to establishing the Economic and Management System (*Sistema de Dirección y Planificación de la Economía*–SDPE) in Cuba. In its first two years, this journal published only articles by Soviet-bloc writers. By 1980, however, after the Cubans had accumulated some experience of their own with the SDPE, the journal was opened to them as well. In the mid-1980s, more Cuban journals appeared, such as *El Economista, Cuba Económica Planificada*, and *Temas de Economía Mundial.*

Although each of these journals had its own characteristics, they all shared a focus on practical matters, whether professional or economic. A typical issue of *Economía y Desarrollo*, for example, featured an "Académicas" section, announcing academic conferences, essay contests, special courses, visiting foreign professors, and Cubans studying abroad; a "Cuba Económica" section, giving detailed information on particular industries, on the economy's overall performance in a particular year, and the like; official speeches and documents of economic relevance; and articles that might range from low-level guidelines for managers to highly technical economic analyses. None of these journals carried sharp or extended debates, or anything like the "Great Debate" that raged in the journals of the 1960s. These journals focused not on discussing the bigger questions of socialist construction but on orienting Cuba's growing numbers of economic professionals to the practical details of the path of socialist construction chosen by the leadership.

Perhaps the most dramatic development for economic professionals in this period was the creation of the National Association of Cuban Economic Professionals (*Asociación Nacional de Economistas de Cuba*—ANEC), which, founded in 1979 with 6,000 members, had grown to some 13,000 members by 1986.[24] ANEC's constitution stated a variety of objectives for the organization: to educate its members about the economic problems of the third world, the economic experiences of the Soviet-bloc countries, and the crisis of the world capitalist system; to help spread economic knowledge and awareness of Cuban economic realities to other professionals and to the trade unions; to maintain relations with foreign professional associations, and to send delegations to international conferences.[25]

This latter required not only reaching out to economic professionals in other countries but also improving the quality of those in Cuba. Soon after ANEC's founding, some Cuban economic professionals noted with embarrassment that, at the Sixth Congress of the International Economics Association, held in Mexico in 1980, a high-level official of the organization had objected to the presence of the Cubans, because they had professionally published little or nothing.[26] Another Cuban economic professional pointed with chagrin to the poor performance of the Cuban delegation to the Second Congress of the Association of Third World Economists, held in Havana in 1981. In his view, the Cuban delegation suffered from

> timidity, a product of lack of experience in the debate of papers and including, in some cases, perplexity before evidence for which we have not always formed our own indispensable criteria, and about which we are not always as systematic in our study as is required in order to present ourselves properly at international events. ... [We have] a certain unconscious tendency to limit ourselves, even when it is not strictly necessary nor convenient, to a narrow area of possibilities in a chosen activity and, therefore, to measure

ourselves inadvertently by what we ourselves generate, which signifies, in fact, that we treat ourselves with extreme benevolence.[27]

To overcome these problems, ANEC was urged to work toward making more information available to Cuban economic professionals and creating conditions for more of them to collectively examine and debate common problems and aspirations with economic professionals from other countries.

ANEC's overriding objective in this period, however, was to help orient economic professionals to the SDPE, which Cuba was then adapting from the Soviets. The SDPE required a large body of economically trained or at least economically aware professionals, first, to apply it and, then, to run it in Cuban conditions. Although the leadership had discussed the SDPE as early as 1973, the economic studies curriculum in higher education was not adjusted to train students to operate the SDPE until the 1977 to 1978 academic year, and the first class fully schooled in the new curriculum was not graduated until 1982. Economic professionals who left school prior to 1982 presumably lacked some skills required by the SDPE, or even an adequate understanding of the system. By bringing those economic professionals who were not trained in the SDPE into a single organization with those who were, ANEC aimed to focus all of the country's economic professionals on the practical problems of implementing the SDPE in Cuba.

The appropriate degree of specialization required of Cuba's economic professionals under the SDPE was one such problem. Until the late 1970s, revolutionary Cuba's schools of higher economic studies focused on training generalists and offered only a couple of academic specialties.[28] As the Cubans began to introduce the SDPE, however, they also introduced—probably copying from Soviet practice at the time—more specialized economic curricula. Beginning with the 1977 to 1978 academic year, students at the various institutes of economy could specialize in accounting, finances and credit, economic policy, national planning, statistics, economy of work, economy of technical-material supply, economy of transportation, and economy of foreign trade. Industrial engineering students in higher polytechnic institutes could further specialize in organization of work, organization of production, and quality control, all with much economic content. Students could specialize in economic studies of tourism at Matanzas University, in agricultural economy at the superior institutes of agricultural sciences, and in management of the socialist economy at the superior institutes of management of the economy.[29]

Such a level of specialization may have been appropriate in the Soviet Union, where economic personnel were relatively plentiful. But Cuba's economic professionals began complaining, through ANEC and such professional journals as *Economía y Desarrollo*, that this level of specialization did not fit their country's conditions. They argued that, given its continuing scarcity of economically trained personnel, Cuba needed not economic specialists but generalists who could deal with a variety of problems in different occupational posts, and who could move from one to another as needed. As a result of such considerations, by the early 1980s higher economic studies in Cuba had begun to retreat, at least partly, from the specialization of the late 1970s.[30]

After 1970, then, Cuba's economic professionals became increasingly active in helping to formulate, evaluate, and implement the policies chosen by the revolutionary leadership. But, as pointed out above, the leaders never envisioned— through ANEC, journals, or any other vehicles—anything like the "Great Debate" of the 1960s; economic professionals were expected to stop short of questioning the leadership's policies.

Because it is one of the clearest and most extended expressions of this expectation, the statement made in 1977 by Humberto Pérez as head of JUCEPLAN is worth quoting at length. Speaking to students and faculty at the University of Havana's Institute of Economy about the type of research they should pursue in relation to the SDPE, Pérez explained:

> Of course, this work of yours should take place with full freedom. ... Not only should you investigate or examine or submit to analysis that about which there has been no official pronouncement or about which you hear that for the moment no idea of making an official pronouncement exists, but you should also submit to study and examine those questions about which official pronouncements have been produced. ... Within the official pronouncements there are questions of principle and questions of how to implement these principles. About questions of principle, of course, about an elemental question of revolutionary discipline, neither seminars should be held or investigations made. But about questions of how to implement these principles, a form of aid to their better implementation is precisely that you examine, without limitations of any type, the implementation already made, even when these principles have the character of a law, of a decree, of a resolution of a Ministry, of a promulgation of any other type.[31]

For the revolutionary leadership, moreover, this defined the decision-making role not of just economic but of all new professionals: They were not supposed to question the leadership's decisions, but they were expected to help formulate, evaluate, and implement those decisions.

Cuba's leaders, however, were not content simply to define the new professionals' decision-making role in relation to their own; they also wanted to shape the new professionals' political consciousness in general. The leadership wanted new professionals who would refrain from trying to parlay their skill and knowledge advantages into material privileges, or from arrogating to themselves, as experts, the right to make decisions bureaucratically without popular participation, ignoring the interests or expressed desires of the regime's popular base. The revolutionary leadership hoped to shape new professionals with a revolutionary—not an elitist, technocratic, or bureau-cratic—consciousness, new professionals who were also "new persons" committed to democratic centralist principles.

To shape such new professionals after 1970, the revolution-ary leadership relied first and foremost on combining study with work (*estudio-trabajo*) in Cuban education. This idea of combining work and study stemmed from the writings of Karl Marx and of the nineteenth-century Cuban revolutionary leader José Martí. Marx, of course, emphasized the need to overcome the social and psychological separation of manual and mental work in order to create an egalitarian society of fully developed human beings. Martí put forth similar ideas, often phrased in poetic prose: "In countries such as ours there must be a thoroughgoing revolution in education if we do not wish to see them—as some are already—perpetually distorted, wasted, and deformed, like the Horatian monster—with a gigantic head and an immense heart, trailing its flagging feet, its withered arms all skin and bones."[32]

Work-study was first declared a principle of Cuban educa-tion in 1964: Resolution 392 of that year called for educational programs that would combine "physical labor with intellectual work, and both of these with life."[33] Beginning in the early 1960s, secondary school students were periodically mobilized to work in industry or agriculture on weekends, holidays, or when demand for labor was particularly high, as during the sugar harvest. In 1966, as the whole society mobilized to expand sugar production, the "school to the countryside" program was born. In this program, analogous to voluntary labor in the rest of the society, secondary students and their teachers travelled to the countryside to engage in various types of agricultural work for a period of thirty-five days a year.[34]

But not until after 1970 did the revolutionary leadership systematically apply the work-study principle to Cuban education. Work-study was then introduced to all levels of the regular educational system, even at the primary level, where students began tending school gardens and helping clean and care for their schools.[35] The farthest-reaching application of work-study, nevertheless, was at the secondary and higher levels of education, responsible for training the new professionals.

In 1971, the National Congress of Education and Culture concluded that the mobilizations of the 1960s had neither involved all secondary school students nor systematically combined work and study. Instead, these mobilizations had frequently interrupted the course of academic studies and hurt academic performance. These mobilizations, moreover, were isolated events—too episodic and too short to instill a "new person" mentality. As a Cuban teacher later explained to me, for the students in these programs, "work and study remained separate, even contradictory, realms."[36]

Despite these criticisms, in 1973 to 1974 the "school to the countryside" program was generalized to the entire regular secondary school system. But except for vocational and technical schools, where the curriculum already combined work with study, this was considered a transitional measure. For basic secondary and preuniversity schools—the training grounds for the bulk of the new professionals—the curriculum was more general and academic; there, the "school *to* the countryside" program would be replaced by "schools *in* the countryside."

Students would board at schools in the countryside during the week and return home on weekends. The school day would be divided into two shifts, one for study and the other for agricultural work on the state farm where the school was located. Students, organized into work brigades according to their year in school, would spend three hours of each school day doing agricultural work. Each school would ordinarily house about 500 students who, along with a regular adult labor force, would be responsible for a little over 500 hectares of state farm land, usually devoted to tobacco, citrus fruits, or other foods. Each task performed by the student work brigades would have output norms, set at about half the productivity rate of a normal adult worker.[37]

These schools would attempt to instill a producer's rather than a consumer's consciousness in their students, making them aware and appreciative of the work and skill that ordinary producers devote to every item of consumption. In addition, it was hoped that, by actually seeing their work bear fruit in an agricultural product, students would learn to value and find joy in work. Finally, these schools were designed to familiarize urban students with the agricultural basis of the country's heritage and society, and to instill in them a respect for the rural population and its critical role in Cuba's economic development. In short, the schools in the countryside were to turn new professionals-in-training, during their formative teen-age years, into "new persons."[38]

Schools in the countryside, of course, could fully achieve this goal only if they were attended by a sizable share of secondary students. While the number of secondary students attending schools in the countryside grew steadily, from 3,438 in 1971 to 1972 to 283,544 in 1980 to 1981, the proportion of secondary students in schools in the countryside grew from 1.7 percent in 1970 to 1971 to 37.7 percent in 1977 to 1978—but then fell to 33.9 percent by the 1980 to 1981 year.[39] This was most likely the result of rapidly increasing enrollments coupled with the costs of building and maintaining these schools in the countryside, which had proven more expensive than initially projected.[40] It might also have been an instance of political goals—in this case, to form new professionals with a revolutionary consciousness—falling victim to economic considerations; as Chapter 6 explains, this happened all too often in the early 1980s.

As at the secondary level, in the 1960s work-study in higher education failed to truly combine work and study.[41] After 1970, however, the work-study principle was applied systematically in higher education. First, greater numbers of correspondence and evening courses, and even university teaching units within work centers, were created for workers and administrative personnel with regular jobs who had completed their secondary education. In the 1960s, such students were relatively few, but by the 1979 to 1980 academic year they numbered 110,988, or 54.4 percent of total higher education enrollments.[42]

Second, in 1971 Fidel Castro announced the first systematic program of work-study for students in the regular higher education system. This new program incorporated four hours of work into each school day, Monday through Friday. Initially, students spent twenty hours a week at work, twenty in classes, and twenty in individual or collective study; beginning in 1977 to 1978, study time was increased to between thirty and thirty-six hours per week.[43]

The most dramatic change that this program underwent in its first few years, however, concerned not study but the type of work combined with it. The question was posed: Should the new professionals-in-training be required to engage in base work (*trabajo de base*), that is, manual or physical work on the shop floor and in the fields, or in specialized work (*trabajo especializado*), that is, nonmanual work in their specialties? One empirical study came out strongly in favor of base work;

the authors claimed it best overcame the manual-mental distinction in the minds of students, who, without the experience, might begin to consider themselves "better" than workers.[44] But although base work predominated in the first few years of the new program, it was soon replaced totally with specialized work. In 1975, the First Congress of the Communist Party of Cuba officially endorsed this change: work at the higher education level was to be "related essentially to professional formation."[45]

Base work was rejected, no doubt, because it came too close to the *modus operandi* of the widely criticized *fidelista* model that was then being jettisoned. Base work also was probably not as effective as specialized work for reinforcing the skills that students were supposed to acquire and for socializing them into their future intermediate-level roles in the democratic centralist decision-making process. In an apparent attempt to help overcome the manual-mental distinction without resorting to base work, in 1973 the revolutionary leadership instituted a period of social service (*servicio social*) for all higher education graduates, requiring them to work in rural areas or in other third world countries for a period of two to three years upon graduation.[46]

In whatever form, the new work-study system was rapidly implemented. As early as the 1972 to 1973 academic year, 95 percent of the students at the University of Havana were involved in the program. Once a series of initial problems were ironed out, work-study was credited with beneficially affecting the new professionals-in-training: the system reportedly had begun to help raise their discipline, promotion rate, and political consciousness.[47]

Still, the revolutionary leadership did not fully succeed in shaping new professionals committed to democratic centralist practice. As we will see in Chapter 6, some new professionals could be found among those who arrogated to themselves the right to make decisions bureaucratically without popular participation. Nor did the revolutionary leadership fully succeed in forming new professionals who would refrain from trying to turn their skill and knowledge advantages into material privileges. Speaking before the Union of Young Communists in 1982, Fidel Castro offered a striking example:

> Mention was made at this congress of the lust for gain, and I think it is important to do so. I mean the lust for gain on the part of some professionals … like the case of an engineer, an architect, or whatever, trained by the revolution, privately practicing his profession and charging exorbitant fees for drawing up simple plans for home repairs. An ad in *Opina* … said: "Home repairs drawn up." A citizen comes to City Hall and is asked to present a plan for home repairs. An urbanization office, or what have you, asked for a little plan. The man charges 800, 900, 1,000 pesos for drawing up a little plan. … That's robbery being committed by a technician trained by the revolution.[48]

This particular abuse was curbed by having municipalities draw up such plans,[49] but the general problem remained. In 1986, Castro castigated the new professional teachers who for pay had privately tutored students, so they could advance faster than others who could not afford such services. He also berated the new professional physicians who had sold medical excuses to workers, so they could receive sick pay or early retirement, and then either not work or work privately for extra money.[50]

These abuses were dealt with by the legal system and, in the case of medicine, also by professional oversight panels, which were set up in 1989.[51]

As Fidel Castro always made clear, only a minority of new professionals ever engaged in such abuses. But he also expressed the fear that, if not stopped, such practices might have spread and corrupted greater numbers of professionals; he

worried, furthermore, that these practices might have corrupted or demoralized workers, and undermined their commitment to hard work and their support for the revolutionary
leadership and even for socialism itself. In 1986 the revolutionary leadership launched another rectification drive (see Chapter 7), which aimed to curb those, whether new professionals
or others, pursuing material privileges, as well as those engaging in the bureaucratic behaviors described in the next chapter.

Notes

1. Orlando Carnota, "Algunas ideas para mejorar el trabajo de
   dirección," *Economía y Desarrollo* 16 (January/February 1973):
   62–93. For other examples of this genre, some of which reach
   a slightly higher level of sophistication, see Emilio Fernández
   Caballero, "El tiempo del dirigente," *Economía y Desarrollo* 18
   (July/August 1973): 92–111, and "Formación de cuadros,"
   Economía y Desarrollo 27 (January/February 1975): 111–35;
   Nery Suarez Lugo, "Notas sobre la evaluación de cuadros,"
   Economía y Desarrollo 34 (October/December 1976): 117–37.
2. Osvaldo Dorticós, "Formación de cuadros económicos-administrativos en la industria ligera," *Economía y Desarrollo* 4
   (October/December 1970): 17.
3. Fernández Caballero, "El tiempo," pp. 101–102.
4. Ibid., p. 108.
5. Humberto Pérez, *Sobre las dificultades objectivas de la
   revolución: lo que el pueblo debe saber* (Havana: Editorial
   Política, 1979), p. 14.
6. Proportions are impossible to determine, and I have heard
   conflicting testimony: Author's interviews SMT.80, AG01.8l, ST2
   .80, CMS.80, and HITS.80.
7. Raúl Castro, "Three Speeches Against Bureaucracy," in Michael
   Taber (ed.), *Fidel Castro Speeches, Vol. 2: Our Power Is That of
   the Working People* (New York: Pathfinder Press, 1983), p. 290.
8. Ibid.
9. "Sobre la política de formación, selección, ubicación, promoción y

superación de los cuadros," in Primer Congreso del Partido Comunista de Cuba, *Tesis y resoluciones* (Havana: Editorial de Ciencias Sociales, 1978), pp. 57-91. Also, see "Resolution on Cadre Training, Selection, Placement, Promotion and Advancement Policy," in Second Congress of the Communist Party of Cuba, *Documents and Speeches* (Havana: Political Publishers, 1981), pp. 297-300; Fernández Caballero, "El tiempo," and Suarez Lugo, "Notas."

10. "Sobre la política de formación," p. 61.

11. "Fifth Congress of the Communist Youth League (UJC)," *Granma Weekly Review*, 12 April 1987, p. 5; and "Deferred Session of the Fifth Central Committee Plenum," *Granma Weekly Review*, 4 October 1987, p. 5.

12. Fidel Castro, "Speech on the Thirty-Fifth Anniversary of the Attack on the Moncada," *Granma Weekly Review*, 7 August 1988, p. 4.

13. The estimate of 532,980 secondary school graduates by 1980 fits nicely with other available data from the same time period. First, as would be expected, the figure falls below the 1979 figure of 844,300 for all employees, including old cadres, in nonmanual occupations. See Comité Estatal de Estadísticas, Dirección de Demografia, *Encuesta demografia nacional de 1979: principales características laborales de la población de Cuba* (Havana: 1981), p. 51. Second, as would be expected, 532,980 is less than the 1979 figure of 746,928 for Cuban labor force participants with "at least twelve years of schooling," which, as explained in the note to Table 5.2, includes individuals without secondary degrees. The 746,928 figure is the author's calculation from data provided by Claes Brundenius, "Some Notes on the Development of Cuban Labor Force 1979-80," Cuban Studies/Estudios Cubanos, 13, no. 2 (Summer 1983): 70, 74.

14. The figure of 147,150 is the author's computation from data given in Brundenius, "Some Notes," pp. 70, 74. Due to lack of data on the number of graduates from certain higher education institutions, such as the Communist Party's Nico López School, it is impossible to use the method of Table 5.2 to estimate accurately the number of higher education graduates remaining in Cuba.

15. The 844,300 figure is from Comité Estatal de Estadísticas,

Encuesta demografia nacional de 1979, p. 51. The category used in this source is "non-manual occupations," which is close to but not the same as my category of "intermediate-level occupations" because, for one thing, "non-manual" includes the revolutionary leadership. Unfortunately, these data offer no way to separate out the revolutionary leaders. But since, at the very most, they might number 0.5 percent of the population, or about 5,000 individuals, the resultant distortion is negligible.

16. Cited in Marc Frank, *Cuba Looks to the Year 2000* (New York: International Publishers, 1993), p. 64.

17. Ibid., p. 62.

18. This latter estimate rests on the assumption that the "not specified" category from Table 5.3 is equivalent to the "no formal education" category given in the source for Table 5.4. Since the "no formal education" category is missing in the data for Table 5.3, this is a distinct possibility, but, of course, cannot be verified.

19. Brundenius, "Some Notes": 72.

20. Federación de Mujeres Cubanas, *Cuban Women in Higher Education* (Havana: Editorial Letras Cubanas, 1985), p. 21 [English translation].

21. Ibid., p. 24.

22. Myriad examples are supplied in the excellent work by Dalton, "Everything Within the Revolution": Cuban Strategies for Social Development Since 1960 (Boulder, CO: Westview Press, 1993).

23. Raúl León Torras, "Clausura del acto central por el Día del Economistas," Economía y Desarrollo 71 (November/December 1982): 244.

24. For the membership figures, see Joaquín Benavides Rodríguez, "Discurso en el acto central por el Día del Economista," *El Economista* 2, no. 3 (December 1986): 11.

25. Asociación Nacional de Economistas de Cuba, "Constitución," *Economía y Desarrollo* 52 (March/April 1978): 27-28.

26. Alexis Codina Jiménez and Joaquín Fernández, "Apuntes en el XX aniversario del inicio de la formación de economistas," *Economía y Desarrollo* 71 (November/December 1982): 37.

27. Torras, "Clausura del acto," pp. 235-36. For this congress, whose major topic was the "Economic Crisis and its Effects upon the Third World," see *Memoirs: Second Congress of the Association of Third*

World Economists (Havana: Editorial de Ciencias Sociales, 1982). Although the research of Cuban economic professionals on the international economy is beyond the scope of this discussion, it should be said that their work has at times been impressive. For representative examples, see the publication of the Center for the Investigation of the World Economy, *Temas de Economía Mundial*; and Fidel Castro's work, *The World Economic and Social Crisis* (Havana: The Council of State, 1983), written with the help of the Center and of the University of Havana's Institute of Economy.

28. *Economía y Desarrollo* 5 (January/March 1971): 196; and *Economía y Desarrollo* 8 (October/December 1971): 222-25.

29. Codina Jiménez and Fernández, "Apuntes," pp. 25-27.

30. See Carlos Rafael Rodríguez, *Palabras en los setenta* (Havana: Editorial de Ciéncias Sociales, 1984), pp. 35-39; and Fernando Vecino Alegret, "La educación superior: sus objetivos y los metodos para lograrlos," *Cuba Socialista* 4-5 (December 1982-February 1983): 3-33.

31. Humberto Pérez, "La obtención de la mayor eficiencia posible en el uso de nuestro recursos," *Economía y Desarrollo* 46 (March/April 1978) 167-69; for a less directive but similar statement made in 1986, see Benavides Rodríguez, "Discurso," pp. 5-12.

32. Quoted in Max Figueroa et al., *The Basic Secondary School in the Countryside: An Educational Innovation in Cuba* (Paris: UNESCO, 1974), p. 9.

33. Quoted in ibid., p. 11.

34. For this historical background, see Figueroa, pp. 10-12; and UNCTAD, *Health and Educational Technology in Cuba* (New York: United Nations Organization, 1979), pp. 22-23.

35. See Karen Wald, *Children of Che* (Palo Alto, CA: Ramparts Press, 1978), p. 180.

36. Author's interview ST2.80.

37. Figueroa, *Basic Secondary School*, pp. 28, 41.

38. For these and other goals of these schools, see ibid., pp. 14-26.

39. Ministerio de Educación, *Informe*, pp. 344-46.

40. CEPAL, *Cuba: estilo de desarrollo y políticos sociales* (Cerro del Agua, México: Siglo Veintiuno Editores, 1980), p. 97.

41. For an overview of work-study in higher education in the 1960s,

see Ministerio de Educación, *El principio de la combinación del trabajo en la educación superior: informe a la conferencia de ministros de educación superior de países socialistas* (Havana: 1974), pp. 26-35.

42. Duchesne, "Superación professional," *Bohemia,* 23 January 1981, p. 35.

43. Ministerio de Educación, *El principio,* p. 39; and Kolesnikov, *Cuba,* p. 191.

44. Niurka Pérez and Elena Díaz, "Primera experiencia de inserción laboral en la facultad de ciencias: estudio exploratoria," *Sobre Educación Superior,* January/June 1975, pp. 60-62.

45. Primer Congreso, p. 386.

46. For information on this social service requirement, see Luís Rodríguez Balmaseda, "El servicio social: una positiva experiencia en la vida graduado," *Bohemia,* 13 August 1982; and "Dictan regulaciones sobre facilidades para graduados que cumplen el servicio social," *Trabajadores,* 13 August 1985.

47. Ministerio de Educación, *El principio,* pp. 39-42, 49-50; and Elena Pérez and Niurka Pérez, "Estudio sobre la integración estudiantil a los centros trabajo," *Sobre Educación Superior,* January/June 1975, pp. 77-92.

48. Fidel Castro, "Revolutionary Consciousness and the Fight Against Corruption," in Michael Taber (ed.), *Fidel Castro Speeches, Vol. 2: Our Power Is That of the Working People* (New York: Pathfinder Press, 1983), p. 341.

49. In 1982, Castro made the suggestion that this be done, and he verified in 1986 before the National Assembly that it was being done. See *Granma Weekly Review,* 12 January 1986, p. 7.

50. For these examples, see *Granma Weekly Review,* 6 July 1986, p. 3; and 13 July 1986, p. 9.

51. Dalton, *"Everything Within the Revolution,"* p. 50.

Chapter 6

Democratic and Bureaucratic Centralism in the Cuban Economy Up to 1986

After 1970, as the Cuban revolution attempted its first rectification while integrating with the Soviet bloc internationally, it scored a variety of social and economic successes. As noted, the post-1970 expansion and transformation of the educational system generally upgraded the population's skills. There were also many other indicators of the revolution's achievements not widely known to the U.S. public.

From 1970 to 1984, for example, average daily caloric intake rose from 2,565 to 2,963; from 1970 to 1984, infant mortality dropped from thirty-nine to fifteen deaths per thousand live births; between 1970 and 1980, although agricultural production grew a moderate 27 percent, industrial production grew a dramatic 80 percent; between 1972 and 1981, according to the estimates of Swedish economist Claes Brundenius, the annual growth rate in gross domestic product averaged 7.8 percent, while the per capita rate averaged a substantial 6.5 percent.[1] The list could go on indefinitely.

Still, the revolution had problems. In 1986, Fidel Castro would exclaim: "As far as salaries go, there is chaos all over the country."[2] And as he and others made clear throughout that year, more was involved than salaries. Prices, credit, employment practices, administrative procedures, and many other aspects of the economy could be characterized as "chaotic."

Beneath this seeming chaos, however, were identifiable patterns of behavior distorting the operation of the post-1970 system. Old cadres, new professionals, many workers, and even revolutionary leaders were interacting with one another in ways that could best be described as bureaucratic centralist, not democratic centralist. At least until 1986, when the revolutionary leadership launched another rectification drive that targeted it and other problems, bureaucratic centralist behavior plagued the Cuban economy.[3]

Socialist theoreticians over the years have coined many terms for behavior deviating from democratic centralist principles and practice. Among these terms, "bureaucratic centralism" is the most useful for highlighting the relationship of such behavior to democratic centralism. Although bureaucratic centralism refers to many different behaviors, they all fall into one of two broad categories depending on where they occur in the three-step process, which was explained in Chapter 4, for making and implementing decisions.

One category of behaviors arises in the second step of this process, where leaders are supposed to make a decision. More general or more important decisions are supposed to be made by higher-level leaders; less general or less important decisions, by lower-level leaders. Here, bureaucratic centralism takes place when higher-level leaders unduly interfere with the responsibilities formally delegated to subordinate leaders. The immediate effect of such interference can be either "malign," as when higher-level leaders usurp the resources or decision-making power of lower levels, or "benign," as when higher-level leaders, by favoring certain lower levels, relieve them of responsibility for their problems.

The other set of behaviors occurs in the first and third steps of the process. In the first step, the lower levels, down to the base, are supposed to collectively discuss the issue at hand; in the third step, these levels are to participate actively in implementing decisions. Hence, bureaucratic centralism occurs here when higher levels unduly interfere with lower-level participation in either the pre-decision-making step of discussion or the post-decision-making step of implementation. Again, the immediate effect can be either "malign," as when higher levels obstruct lower-level participation, or "benign," as when higher levels gain lower-level cooperation not through discussion but through favors.

The concepts of democratic and bureaucratic centralism, of course, are too general to determine at what point higher-level interference becomes *undue.* This can only be determined by analyzing the character and effects of higher-level interference in particular instances. Despite their generality, however, the concepts of democratic and bureaucratic centralism provide a framework to guide the following analysis of specific events in the Cuban economy, a framework that helps illuminate the connections among seemingly unrelated, contradictory, or chaotic patterns of behavior.

Undue Interference in Lower-level Decision-making and Responsibilities

In Cuba, at least prior to 1986, bureaucratic centralism began at the very pinnacle of the revolutionary leadership with Fidel Castro himself, and from there rippled down through all levels of the economic system. Castro often spoke about his personal interventions to detect and solve problems at all levels of the economy; he frequently explained that his staff of "twenty *compañeros* ... constantly travel, visiting factories, hospitals, schools, *coordinating, helping everybody,* and they are not inspectors but people who go around assessing the situation and *coordinating one organ with another.*[4] Although Castro boasted elsewhere about the smallness of his staff,[5] the issue here is not its size but the character of its work. The attempt to coordinate *everybody* from the pinnacle in an ad hoc way is a bureaucratic centralist mode of operation par excellence.

This is made clear by the particularly harsh description of Castro's interventions offered by an emigre Cuban manager:

> After he visits a production unit conditions and results improve for a while. He puts his finger on the sore spot. It is Fidel's command, and the party cell means nothing, the organizational structure means nothing. Whatever Fidel says must be done. ... Within a week of his visit to the Antillana steel mill, 1,200 bicycles and twenty buses were allocated to the plant. Who could do this but Fidel? ... Fidel erodes all economic plans, he destroys them. He flouts any plan in order to resolve a given problem in the place he is visiting. The problem is fixed in a few days but it will crop up again within three or four months.[6]

The claim that even the preeminent revolutionary leader destroys *all* economic plans is clearly an exaggeration. Yet this statement begins to highlight some of the consequences of this type of bureaucratic centralism. Such interventions might have a benign, if short-term, impact on a particular location. But one need only wonder where the 1,200 bicycles and twenty buses came from to realize that their loss might have a malign impact elsewhere.

Bureaucratic centralism, however, was not limited to Castro and his twenty *compañeros.* It was also evident throughout the Cuban economy, especially in the relationship between the higher state organs, most particularly the ministries, and the enterprises subordinated to them. As was seen in Chapter 5, with the introduction of the new Economic Management and Planning System (SDPE) in the late 1970s, enterprises were to become semi-autonomous units. By 1980, however, it was evident that ministries would not easily allow their enterprises the autonomy envisioned, and many complaints about "excessive" ministerial "tutelage and paternalism" began to be voiced.[7] "[W]hile the central planning system reduces its directive indicators [to enterprises]," reported the Communist Party newspaper in 1985, "the ministries increase them, and the intent of the reform is lost in excessive paternalism."[8]

Ministries were treating their enterprises bureaucratically in a variety of ways. They were demanding excessive information from their enterprises, for example, in order to keep close tabs on their operation. In 1980, Felino Quesada Pérez of the Central Planning Agency (JUCEPLAN) stated that, as of 1979, almost two-thirds of the SDPE enterprises were being directed to collect and hand over statistical data that were not required by the National System of Statistical Information.[9] Fully 75 percent of these directives came from central state organizations, mostly the ministries.[10] The situation had little improved by 1986, when Fidel Castro complained that "statistics continued to be a mountain of data of debatable usefulness."[11] Quesada Pérez underscored that the collection and dissemination of such statistics wasted both time and material resources, and deflected enterprise personnel from their proper concerns; he pointedly asked, "Can an enterprise overwhelmed with so much information ... really dedicate itself to deepening the analysis of its enterprise management?"[12]

Ministerial bureaucratic centralism, however, was not limited merely to demands for information, but involved undue interference in the finances and daily operation of enterprises. Quesada Pérez gave three telling examples.[13] First, he reported the case of a provincial office of a ministry that, when it found itself without sufficient funds to meet its payroll, illegally extracted 80,000 pesos from the National Bank account of one of the enterprises subordinate to it, at a time when the enterprise owed the bank over 847,000 pesos in overdue loans.

Second, he reported that many enterprise managers complained that ministerial authorities had ordered them not to declare their excess inventories superfluous. Although such ministerial orders lacked legal force, they nevertheless kept these enterprises from selling unneeded material to other enterprises that could use it.

Third, he reported that many enterprise managers were complaining that they could not enter into contracts to sell their products to other enterprises, again because of illegal orders from their ministries. Quesada Pérez reported that "frequently" enterprise managers had asked him: "'When are we going to have real enterprises?' 'When will we have autonomous enterprises?' 'When are we going to be able to make decisions in our enterprises?'"[14]

Despite such complaints, however, the bureaucratic centralism of higher authorities in Cuba did not have only malign consequences for those subjected to it.[15] At the same time that higher authorities hindered enterprises, they also routinely bailed them out of difficulties. Although the SDPE envisioned enterprises that would be financially responsible for themselves and to the National Bank, if enterprises had losses at the end of the year, the National Bank routinely covered them.[16] On the other hand, although SDPE enterprises were supposed to realize a profit within the confines of relatively stable prices, central price authorities were very willing to grant price increases to enterprises. They were so willing, in fact, that in 1986 Fidel Castro warned that the SDPE "could become a complete farce, as regards enterprise efficiency" if enterprises were allowed to continue attempting to solve their problems through price increases.[17]

Moreover, often when enterprise managers could not get

permission from higher authorities to raise prices as high as they would have liked, they resorted to various subterfuges, such as demanding the price of a finished job when supplying only the materials, for gouging other enterprises.[18] In short, partially due to the benign bureaucratic centralism of the central authorities and partially due to the corrupt manipulations of some enterprise managers, at least prior to 1986, both the budget and price constraints on Cuban enterprises were exceedingly soft.[19]

A closer look at the examples provided by Quesada Pérez shows that benign and malign bureaucratic centralism, where higher levels usurped the responsibilities of lower levels, could also interact to subvert the purposes of the SDPE. When enterprises were robbed of funds for operating their plants or for paying their debts, or were prevented from acquiring funds through selling their excess inventories, it strengthened the incentive for their managers to acquire funds by seeking concessions from banking or price authorities. The same was true when enterprises were prevented from entering into contracts to sell their goods: they then sometimes produced goods that no one wanted and that could not be sold; as a result, they could run up debts that could not easily be paid and from which they would try to get excused. Harmful interference by higher authorities, thus, encouraged enterprises to actively seek from them benign bureaucratic centralist remedies in the form of soft budget and price constraints.

In Cuba such weak constraints paved the way for a variety of problems, including labor hoarding, as will be seen in the next section, and corruption. Unrestrictive budget and price constraints facilitated the efforts of some managers and others to divert public resources to their and their buddies' personal ends. The relative abundance of the resources at their disposal not only helped corrupt managers evade detection by the authorities over them, it also helped them avoid overly upsetting their own subordinates.

The case (famous in Cuba) of Silvia Marjorie Spence was perhaps the exception that proves the rule. Spence was fired from her work for complaining about contracts for nonexistent jobs and incredibly high monthly salaries by Cuban standards: one of 1,246 pesos, one of 1,013 pesos, four over 900, and four over 800. Eventually, she was reinstated and her former managers were demoted to the shop floor, but her vindication came only after over two years of constant complaining and only after she had complained directly to the country's top leaders.[20] Given the combination of the soft constraints, the potential for substantial personal gain, and the unlikelihood of getting caught, it is not surprising that, at least up to 1986, such corruption had apparently reached epidemic proportions in Cuba.[21]

Undue Interference in Workers' Participation in Discussing and Implementing Plans

Bureaucratic centralism of the second type, in which higher administrators unduly interfered with the participation of lower-level personnel in pre-decision-making discussions or in post-decision-making implementation could exist at any level of the economy. But in Cuba it was most evident in the enterprises and work centers (local subunits of enterprises) where managers and workers interacted directly.

Although no one has claimed that workers have ever exercised effective control over the higher levels of economic planning in revolutionary Cuba, the scholars who have specifically studied the question all agree that, as a result of the organizational changes detailed in Chapter 4, the right of workers to discuss the basic production issues of their enterprises and work centers increased substantially after 1970.[22] Still, it is clear that, at least before 1986, this form of worker participation did not reach the genuine, if limited, level envisioned for it in the democratic centralist model. As the "Resolution on the Economic Planning and Management System" of the Second Communist Party Congress pointedly explained in 1980:

> It has not been possible to achieve the desired level of workers' participation in the drawing up of plans for enterprises, either because the time for this was not programmed or because the meetings to discuss figures for controlling the plan were not properly organized. In some cases, the administration of the enterprise or local and central agencies failed to provide the workers' collectives with all the necessary information. Then, when the final figures were released, no explanation was given as to why their proposals were not accepted—which was usually due to difficulties with supplies or some technical problem.[23]

It is clear from this that these problems stemmed from the negligence of both higher-level administrative personnel—who failed to provide enterprises with information on time, or at all—and enterprise or work center managers who failed to see to it that time was provided for workers to carry out discussions. The malign bureaucratic centralist behavior of various administrative levels rendered this form of worker participation problematic. Moreover, the failure of workers' participation, even if not characteristic of all places at all times, was general enough to draw attention from party congresses and revolutionary leaders. In 1986, Fidel Castro was still noting that "until recently no progress ... [was] made to facilitate practical participation by all administrative levels and workers' collectives in designing the plan."[24]

As with other forms of bureaucratic centralism, this type was not solely malign. Cuban managers often struck benign bureaucratic deals with workers over the terms of their employment. Managers often offered workers jobs that required less effort overall (while sometimes requiring intense periods of productive effort) and guaranteed an acceptable or even higher rate of pay than alternative employment. As Fidel Castro complained in 1986, managers, facilitated by soft budget and price constraints, had "competed among themselves to get the best workers, paid the best salaries, were less demanding, played the role of populists, paternalists, what have you, making no demands."[25]

There seem to have been two, perhaps interrelated, reasons why managers were so willing to offer such deals. On the one hand, it was suggested in a Cuban debate of these issues that some managers did "not want problems and ... [were] afraid of workers."[26] It is perhaps notable in this regard that some Cuban workers interviewed in the early 1980s felt they had the power to have work center managers removed, if necessary.[27] On the other hand, in Cuba, as in the other socialist economies of the time, something close to full employment was guaranteed and the labor market was tight.[28] As a result, managers faced the problem of attracting and retaining workers who could easily switch to other places of employment. Managers, therefore, probably offered such deals to ensure that their workers were appeased and that their production quotas were met.

The workers involved, of course, were not simply passive recipients of managerial largesse. They actively accepted such managerial offers and remained at their jobs to exert the minimum level of productive effort required. Meanwhile, knowing that some managers feared them and that the labor market was tight, workers actively bargained for better terms of employment. Many workers demanded the benign bureaucratic centralist deals that many managers were willing to offer. As Fidel Castro later put it: "[The] ambition for money, the spirit of profit ... was invading our working class."[29]

In the aggregate and over the long run, such deals operated against the workers' and everyone else's broader interest in greater overall production and economic efficiency. But on the local level and in the short run, such deals helped solve the immediate problem of many managers, and evidently appealed to many, if not all, workers. This form of "workers' participation," at least up to 1986, was quite widespread in Cuba. As Fidel Castro eventually would proclaim, the post-1970 principle of "to each according to work" had been "abused ... by paying for work not done."[30]

The revolutionary leadership had specifically, if not very successfully, attempted to reestablish work norms after 1970, in part to prevent workers from securing full pay for less than acceptable levels of work or even for no work at all. Work norms were supposed to be introduced after 1970 in two phases: The first phase was to put into place "elemental" norms; the second phase, "technical" norms.

Elemental norms were based on records of how much workers had produced on particular jobs in the recent past and on timing workers on these jobs in the present. Since management controlled records of past performance and since workers controlled their speed while being timed, both work center managers and workers exerted considerable influence over the level at which elemental norms were set. At least partially because both managers and workers gained immediate advantage by having these norms set at the lowest possible mark, elemental norms overall were relatively low. They were primarily a device for detecting the effects of production interruptions, rather than for increasing workers' productivity.[31]

Technical norms, by contrast, were to be based on scientific studies, not just of individual jobs, but of work centers, enterprises, and even whole sectors of the economy. These studies were supposed to focus on all factors, such as poor equipment, poor or late supplies, poor maintenance, poor planning, and poor organization of the work process, that negatively affected productivity. Technical norms were meant to be a device for reorganizing work and intensifying labor.[32]

In 1972, then-Minister of Labor Jorge Risquet announced that elemental norming would be complete and extensive technical norming would commence by the end of 1973. Almost a decade later, however, almost 28 percent of the appropriate work posts remained without norms of any kind, 77 percent of all existing norms remained elemental, practically none were technical, and 23 percent were somewhere in between.[33]

The slowness of this process may have resulted from the enormous difficulties of establishing and keeping norms up to date in the face of a complex division of labor and changing technology, work organization, and worker performance; from managerial and worker resistance to technical norms; or from some combination of both. But the fact remains that the first phase of fully introducing elemental norms was never even completed, and the second phase of introducing technical norms was hardly even begun.

A speech delivered by Raúl Castro in 1979 is worth quoting at length for its unusually graphic description of how certain individuals were manipulating work norms:

> The fact is that there are many instances of lack of work discipline, unjustified absences from work, deliberate go-slows so as not to surpass the norms, which are already low and poorly applied in practice, so that they won't be changed because they are being more than met. ... There are a good many instances today, especially in agriculture, of people one way or another pulling one trick or another, ... working no more than four or six hours, with the exception of cane-cutters and possibly a few other kinds of work. We know that, in many cases, heads of brigades and foremen make a deal with them to meet the norm in half a day and then go off

and work for the other half for some nearby small farmer, or to go slow and meet the norm in seven or eight hours; or to do two or three norms in a day and report them over other days, too, days on which they don't go to work, either just to do nothing at all or to do something else that brings in some more money; or to surpass the norm in eight hours but report having worked for ten or twelve hours so as not to have the norm upped. ... All this is detrimental to production, the costs of the enterprise, and the produce that should be meeting the needs of the people. And all these "tricks of the trade" in agriculture are also found in industry, transportation services, repair shops, and many other places where there's rampant buddyism: cases of "you do me a favor and I'll do you one" and pilfering on the side. ... The weaknesses and negligence are the responsibility of managers and of all of us who have not set up the most adequate work and salary mechanism and have not known how to organize things and create a certain sense of political and work responsibility on the part of workers.[34]

Such manipulations played havoc with the principle of "to each according to work" and threatened to make the official wage scales meaningless. Low elemental norms often enabled workers to rack up sizeable bonuses, and to thereby gain salaries equivalent to or greater than those of more highly educated workers and even of intermediate-level professionals who were at higher notches on the official wage scales.

One study of eighty-five enterprises in Ciego de Ávila province, for example, discovered that 2,442 were being overpaid due to the low work norms in thirty-two enterprises, in twenty-eight of which workers were regularly producing at a rate more than 130 percent of their norms.[35] This, of course, operated as a disincentive for workers to advance up the official wage scales by improving their educational levels; it also probably demoralized some new professionals who saw workers with less education earning more than themselves.

In the words of one member of the revolutionary leadership, "the correct organization and norming of work, even in the elemental phase, should guarantee that disproportionate salaries that result in a disharmony and dislocation of the entire system are not produced."[36] Yet such disharmony was inherent in the system of elemental norms. One roundabout way to mitigate this problem would have been to stretch official wage scales, as was done in 1980, to increase the distance between the base wages for different levels of jobs. But to eliminate the problem in this way would have required raising wages for higher-level jobs far beyond what the revolutionary leadership ever suggested and probably beyond what the Cuban people would have easily tolerated.

Low elemental norms, by requiring each worker to work very little, also encouraged managers to hoard labor as a way of ensuring that enough labor would be performed in their economic unit to meet production quotas at critical points. As Fidel Castro observed in 1986: "There's often a tendency, instead of going and telling the worker 'make a greater effort, meet your obligation'... to go about making things up, asking for more people."[37] The incentive for managers to hoard labor was particularly high when benign bureaucratic centralism in the form of soft budget and price constraints enabled managers to excessively expand their economic unit's total wage bill.

The machinations reported by Raúl Castro arose when elemental norms were used, or rather abused. But in many instances managers apparently did not even use these norms, except to complete some critical link in the production process or to fulfill a delayed plan. For the most part, managers reverted to paying workers by time, not work performed—especially in slow periods when there was little work to be done or in idle periods when production was interrupted because of weather, shortage of supplies, or lack of managerial foresight. Managers guaranteed workers their base wage as determined by their position on the official wage scale, regardless of how much they actually produced.[38]

Alternatively, many managers took advantage of the Cuban labor law that guaranteed workers 70 percent of their official wages, paid by the state, in the event of temporary layoffs made necessary by production interruptions. Such managers used this proviso to pay workers for longer periods of time and maintain a surplus labor force, that is, to hoard labor as protection against the vagaries of the tight labor market.[39] In order to keep workers attached to their economic units, many managers saw to it that workers got paid, not for work performed according to norm, but simply for being on the payroll, available when needed.

To recapitulate, the malign bureaucratic centralism of administrative personnel inhibited the ability of Cuban workers to participate in discussing the basic production issues of their enterprises and work centers. Although greater than it had been in the 1960s, this participation suffered at least up to 1986. Cuban workers, however, were able to participate widely in negotiating the terms of employment with managers. Meanwhile, though they sometimes feared workers or needed to attract and retain them in Cuba's tight labor market, managers were willing to offer workers deals that demanded less work at acceptable or even higher pay than alternative employment. In this way, at least up to 1986, a pattern of benign bureaucratic centralism was established in Cuba between many managers and many workers.

Some Major Causes of Bureaucratic Centralism

All socialist economies that have existed have suffered from bureaucratic centralism, which can be explained in part, therefore, by "systemic" factors, inherent in the structure and operation of those economies. Still, the incidence and intensity of bureaucratic centralism has varied among different socialist economies and among different types of economic actors within them at different times. Bureaucratic centralism must in part be explained, therefore, by "sociohistorical" factors that have been present only sometimes. From what has already been said, it is clear that the problem of bureaucratic centralism was quite severe in Cuba, at least up to 1986; and, as will be seen presently, different types of economic actors contributed to this severity for their own, quite different, reasons. Thus, both systemic and sociohistorical factors must be sought to explain Cuba's plague of bureaucratic centralism.

Perhaps the most elaborated theory of the systemic factors behind bureaucratic centralist behavior is that of the Hungarian economist Janos Kornai, who identifies the key systemic factor as the socialist relations of production themselves.[40] The very fact of state ownership of the major means of production, according to Kornai, encourages revolutionary leaders to develop a sense of responsibility for the economy as a whole and for its various units. As a result, the incentive is strong for top leaders to take responsibility at any level of the economy, to intervene even down to the level of a particular work center, when they perceive that actors at these levels are creating or not solving problems, or when they perceive that such actors need help. This does not mean, of course, that each economic unit is equally cared for at each point; some units may be treated malignly in order to benignly help others or to protect wider interests. What is true for revolutionary leaders also holds for managers at every other level of the economy. They are likely to develop for their own economic unit and for the totality of the units subordinated to them a sense of responsibility, similar, although of narrower scope, to that of the top revolutionary leadership.[41]

Kornai brilliantly explicates the connections between bureaucratic centralism and typical socialist economic patterns: full employment in society together with overemployment in enterprises, high rates of investment together with scarcities of consumer goods, etc., before his argument starts to weaken. He interprets his most fundamental proposition, that bureaucratic centralist behavior stems systemically from the socialist nature of the relations of production, in a strikingly incomplete fashion—treating these relations as if they were not relations at all, as if they involved solely leaders and intermediate-level managers. These sectors, of course, form only one pole of the socialist relations between themselves and the opposite pole: workers.

Kornai overlooks the possibility that to the extent that workers participated in controlling production, bureaucratic centralist interventions from above would become both less likely and less necessary. Malign interventions would conflict with workers' rights over production, and would thereby become less likely; benign interventions would conflict with workers' responsibilities for production, and would thereby become less necessary. Even though the practical question of what institutional or other arrangements would best enable workers to participate effectively in controlling production is far from settled,[42] the theoretical point stands. Consequently, Kornai's fundamental proposition needs to be emended: Bureaucratic centralist behavior stems systemically from state ownership together with insufficient workers' participation in controlling production.

Once bureaucratic centralism exists, its various types interact with one another, and bureaucratic centralism tends to become self-generating and self-reinforcing. As already seen, for example, when enterprises are put in jeopardy by the bureaucratic centralist interference of higher authorities, this strengthens their incentive to request compensatory benign interventions. Also, when higher authorities routinely cover the expenses incurred, they thereby encourage managers to seek protection from the vagaries of a tight labor market (another systemic feature of normally operating socialist economies) by striking benign bureaucratic deals with workers. Moreover, anytime higher-level personnel engage in bureaucratic centralism, they create an example for lower-level personnel to emulate.

But given that bureaucratic centralism arises systemically from state ownership *and* insufficient workers' participation, perhaps the most important self-reinforcing pattern is this: If bureaucratic centralism becomes commonplace, lower-level initiative is stifled and whatever institutional vehicles of workers' participation that may exist become ineffective. This, in turn, leads to further intervention from above. Although he reversed the causal sequence, Raúl Castro once described this connection quite vividly:

> [A]fter ... the process of institutionalization, we are still not able to see to it that every worker and peasant, student or soldier, and every minister of state and party leader knows exactly what his or her powers, obligations, and tasks are. ... . [W]hy do so many pull back when they face problems and limit themselves to telling those nearest at hand that "things are rough" rather than immediately assuming responsibilities, be they those of a simple worker or those of an official or leader at any level? After twenty years of revolution are we going to continue the widespread practice of waiting for somebody to push us to do our duty? Or to be quite clear:

How long are we going to go on allowing unresolved
problems to reach crisis point and then ask Comrade Fidel
to take over the situation and pull our chestnuts out of the
fire?[43]

Of course, Raúl Castro could just as well have asked how
many called or waited for the intervention not just of Comrade
Fidel, but of other members of the revolutionary leadership,
the ministries, the banking, price, and other authorities. For, as
has been seen, although bureaucratic centralism in Cuba
started at the top, it surely did not end there. But the central
point here is that waiting for Fidel or for other members of
the administrative apparatus was clearly different than waiting
for Godot—the former could be expected to show up. And so
long as individuals knew this, they were likely to orient their
behavior to it: they would often wait rather than take initiative,
and their lack of initiative further encouraged higher-level
personnel to intervene in a bureaucratic centralist fashion.

Bureaucratic centralism, then, arose in Cuba partly from the
proximate or mediate impact of systemic factors. But it also
arose from sociohistorical factors.[44] The most obvious such
factor was the multifaceted legacy of the experience of the
1960s, and especially of the *fidelista* period. That era of highly
centralized decision-making, in which workers had little voice,
and in which the watchword was to mobilize for production
rather than to debate problems or alternatives, formed hard-
to-break bureaucratic habits in many administrative personnel.
The last chapter's reference to Humberto Pérez's remark on
the bureaucratic habits of many old cadres could apply as well
to the revolutionary leadership, which, although it encouraged
democratic centralist principles, itself often engaged in bureaucratic centralist behavior.

After 1970 the leadership indicated its genuine desire to
move in a democratic centralist direction—although without

giving up ultimate control through the system of interlocking positions in the Communist Party and other organizations. But in the immediate situation, when problems emerged, the leadership often responded, out of habit, in a bureaucratic centralist way.

Of course, the legacy of the 1960s is embodied most directly in the old cadres who rose to positions of responsibility in that period on the basis of reputations for political reliability rather than educational credentials and skills. Many of them probably chose to shun the participatory parts of the democratic centralist decision-making process. Some did so out of encrusted bureaucratic habit; others, recognizing their own relative lack of skills, simply had no desire to open up their decisions to lower-level and worker scrutiny.

Furthermore, because of their lack of skills, many old cadres have doubtless had difficulty solving their problems without striking benign bureaucratic centralist deals with those below and without seeking bureaucratic centralist help from those above. Although bureaucratic centralist behavior has perhaps not appealed equally to all old cadres, it must have greatly appealed to those old cadres with the most bureaucratic habits and fewest skills.

New professionals have engaged in bureaucratic centralist behavior as well, but in most cases not for the same reasons as old cadres. Compared to the latter, new professionals are more likely to have internalized the principles of democratic centralism, both because of their training and because these principles justify their relative position and role in the decision-making process. Possessing educational credentials and presumed expertise, they no doubt have had more confidence in their decisions, and less fear of opening these up to lower-level scrutiny. With relatively greater skills, they are more likely to be able to solve problems without resorting to bureaucratic interactions with those above and below them, and hence tend to resent bureaucratic centralist interventions from above.

Cuba's new professionals, however, have not been immune to bureaucratic centralism. Not only have they been subject to the same systemic factors as all other Cubans, but also they have had their own reasons for engaging in bureaucratic centralist behavior. As was seen in the last chapter, despite the revolutionary leadership's preventative measures, some new professionals attempted to parlay their skill and knowledge advantages into material privileges. Some have also probably developed, not a revolutionary, but an elitist, technocratic, or bureaucratic consciousness and attempted to arrogate to themselves the right to make decisions bureaucratically without lower-level participation. What has probably pushed some new professionals toward bureaucratic centralist behavior is their very expertise and their consciousness of themselves as experts.

The apparently high incidence and intensity of bureaucuratic centralism that plagued Cuba at least up to 1986, then, resulted from both systemic and sociohistorical factors. Among other things, it resulted from the bureaucratic habits of revolutionary leaders and of old cadres; from the elitist pretensions of new professionals; and from the general absence among workers of a developed sense of their collective rights and collective responsibilities, a sense that would keep them from easily tolerating malign interventions or accepting benign deals. Workers, of course, would likely develop such a sense only if they were allowed to exercise much more control over production than was the case in Cuba, at least up to 1986.

Notes

1. Caloric intake: Figure for 1970 supplied by Eugenio Balari, Director, Instituto Cubano de Investigaciones y Orientación de la Demanda Interna; figure for 1984, from Comité Estatal Estadística, *Anuario Estadístico de Cuba* (Havana: 1984). Infant Mortality: *Granma Weekly Review*, 1 February 1987, p. 1. Output: Gonzalo M. Rodríguez Mesa, "El desarrollo industrial de Cuba y la maduración de inversiones," *Economía y Desarrollo* 68 (May/June 1982), p. 127. Growth: Author's computations from estimates of Claes Brundenius, *Revolutionary Cuba: The Challenge of Growth with Equity* (Boulder, CO: Westview Press, 1984), p. 40.

2. Fidel Castro, "Let the Spirit of Militancy Be the Main Thing We Get Out of This [Third CDR] Congress," *Granma Weekly Review*, 5 October 1986, p. 9.

3. Although the focus here is on the economy, bureaucratic centralist behaviors were evident throughout the Cuban system, including the Organs of Popular Power (OPP). The Second Congress of the Communist Party of Cuba, *Documents and Speeches* (Havana: Political Publishers, 1981), pp. 346-52, after applauding the OPP for being an effective channel of popular participation in the state, noted that greater care had to be taken to ensure that higher bodies did not usurp the responsibilities of lower ones. The best and most detailed available non-Cuban scholarly analysis generally agrees that the OPP, while opening up the Cuban political system to more extensive and stable political participation, has been itself riddled with limitations and problems, many of a bureaucratic centralist nature. See Carollee Bengelsdorf, "Between Vision and Reality: Democracy in Socialist Theory and Practice" (Ph.D. diss., Massachusetts Institute of Technology, 1985).

4. *Granma*, 11 February 1985, pp. 14-15, as quoted in Sergio Roca, "State Enterprises in Cuba Under the New System of Planning and Management (SDPE)," *Cuban Studies/Estudios Cubanos* 16 (1986): 174 (emphasis added).

5. Frei Betto, *Fidel y religión: conversaciones con Frei Betto* (Havana: Consejo de Estado, 1985), p. 39.

6. Quoted in Roca, "State Enterprises," p. 172.

7. *Segunda plenaria nacional de chequeo de la implantación del SDPE* (Havana: Ediciones JUCEPLAN, 1980), p. 405. Also see Julio A. Díaz Vázquez, "La aplicación y perfeccionamiento de los mecanismos de dirección en la economía cubana," *Economía y Desarrollo* 78 (January/February 1984): 94.

8. *Granma*, 16 February 1985, as quoted in Roca, "State Enterprises," pp. 161-62.

9. Felino Quesada Pérez, "La autonomía de la empresa en Cuba y la implantación del sistema de dirección y planificación de la economía," *Cuestiones de la Economía Planificada* 3, no. 1 (January/February 1980): 97.

10. *Segunda plenaria*, pp. 7-8.

11. Fidel Castro, "Main Report to the Third Congress of the Communist Party of Cuba," *Granma Weekly Review*, 16 February 1986, p. 7.

12. Quesada Pérez, "La autonomía," p. 97.

13. Ibid., pp. 97-98. Roca, "State Enterprises," pp. 159-60, reports comparable examples involving ministerial interference with enterprise resources and planning.

14. Quesada Pérez, "La autonomía," pp. 95-96.

15. Sergio Roca, who has written one of the only other studies, cited above, of problems with enterprise autonomy under Cuba's SDPE, mistakenly assumed that higher-level interference typically impacted only negatively on enterprises. Perhaps because he relied solely on the testimony of emigre ex-managers, Roca failed to discover that enterprise managers, as discussed farther on, not only sometimes bristled under malign bureaucratic centralism but sometimes invited benign bureaucratic centralism from those above them, or even needed such interventions because of their irresponsibility.

16. See, for example, Fidel Castro, "Speech at the Twenty-Fifth Anniversary of the Committees for the Defense of the Revolution," *Granma Weekly Review*, 6 October 1985, p. 4; Fidel Castro, "Speech at the Close of the Deferred Session of the Third Congress of the Communist Party of Cuba," *Granma Weekly Review*, 14 December 1986, p. 12; and "Debates on Rectification of Errors and Negative Tendencies in Various Spheres of Society at

the Deferred Session of the Third Congress of the Communist Party of Cuba," *Granma Weekly Review,* 4 December 1986, p. 12.

17. Castro, "Main Report to the Third Congress," p. 7. Roca, "State Enterprises," pp. 162–63, quotes emigre ex-enterprise managers who claimed that price constraints on enterprises were overly harsh in the late 1970s. Perhaps so, but the situation certainly reversed in the 1980s.

18. Castro, "Speech at the Close of the Deferred Session," p. 11; also see his "Speech at the Closing of the Ninth Session of the National Assembly," *Granma Weekly Review,* 12 January 1986, p. 10; and "Report on Fidel Castro's Speech at the Twenty-Fifth Anniversary of the Proclamation of the Socialist Nature of the Revolution," *Granma Weekly Review,* 27 April 1986, p. 10.

19. Hard versus soft budget and price constraints on enterprises are at the center of Janos Kornai's important comparative theory of capitalist and socialist economies, discussed below. See his *Economics of Shortage* (Amsterdam: North-Holland, 1980), chap. 13; and his *Contradictions and Dilemmas* (Cambridge: Massachusetts Institute of Technology Press, 1986), chap. 6.

20. For the details of this case, see "Report on Fidel Castro's Analysis of the Economic Situation and the Essential Measures to Be Taken," *Granma Weekly Review,* 11 January 1987, p. 4; and "New Hero: Whistle-Blower Silvia Majorie Spence," *Cuba Update,* 8, no. 1–2 (Spring 1987): 7. For more on the problem of corruption, see "Report on Fidel Castro's Speech at the Meeting to Analyze Enterprise Management in the City and Province of Havana," *Granma Weekly Review,* 6 July 1986, p. 2; and Castro, "Let the Spirit of Militancy," p. 4.

21. Although clearly secondary to that in the state sector, corruption also became a major problem in areas where centrally controlled price and budget constraints did not operate, such as the free farmers' markets. See Medea Benjamin et al., *No Free Lunch: Food and Revolution in Cuba Today* (San Francisco: Institute for Food and Development Policy, 1984), chap. 5; and Fidel Castro, "Closing Speech at the Second National Meeting of Agricultural Production Cooperatives," *Granma Weekly Review,* 1 June 1986.

22. Andrew Zimbalist, "Workers' Participation in Cuba," *Challenge,* November/December 1975, pp. 45-54; Marifeli Pérez-Stable, "Institutionalization and the Workers' Response," *Cuban Studies/Estudios Cubanos* 6, no. 2 (July 1976): 31-54, and her "Politics and *Conciencia* in Revolutionary Cuba, 1959-1984" (Ph.D. diss., State University of New York at Stony Brook, 1985); Alejandro Amengol Ríos and Ovidio d'Angelo Hernández, "Aspectos de los procesos de comunicación y participación de los trabajadores en la gestión de las empresas," *Economía y Desarrollo* 42 (July/August 1977): 156-79; Antonio José Herrara and Hernan Rosenkranz, "Political Consciousness in Cuba," in John Griffiths and Peter Griffiths (eds.), *Cuba: The Second Decade* (London: Writers and Readers Cooperative, 1979), pp. 36-52; Marta Harnecker, *Cuba: Dictatorship or Democracy?* (Westport, CT: Lawrence Hill, 1980); Linda Fuller, "The Politics of Workers' Control in Cuba, 1959-1983: The Work Center and the National Arena" (Ph.D. diss., University of California at Berkeley, 1985), her "Changes in the Relationship among the Unions, Administration, and the Party at the Cuban Workplace, 1959-1982," *Latin American Perspectives* 13, no. 2 (Spring 1986): 6-32, and her *Work and Democracy in Socialist Cuba* (Philadelphia: Temple University Press, 1992).

23. *Second Congress,* p. 387. For further evidence of these problems, see Hector Ayala Castro, "Transformación de propriedad en el período 1964-1980." *Economía y Desarrollo* 68 (May/June 1982): 23-24; and Díaz Vázquez, "La aplicación," pp. 92-93.

24. Fidel Castro, "Main Report," p. 7.

25. Fidel Castro, "Speech at the Close of the Deferred Session," p. 12.

26. See the remarks of Reinaldo Marsilli, as reported in "Debates on Rectification," p. 3.

27. Fuller, "Politics of Workers' Control," pp. 423-25.

28. Calling the Cuban labor market "tight" does not imply that there was an absolute labor shortage in Cuba. First, a tight labor market can go hand in hand with a labor surplus within all enterprises, or what is sometimes called "unemployment on the job." See Kornai, *Economics,* pp. 30-36 and 254-57. Second, while there was a relative labor shortage in most of Cuba, in fact,

according to Fidel Castro, there was "a certain labor surplus" in Eastern Cuba. See "Report on Fidel Castro's Analysis," p. 4. Interestingly enough, he had complained several months before about the difficulties of a new textile mill in Santiago (that is, in the labor-surplus East) to attract workers, because it did not have the housing, recreational, educational, and other facilities that workers demanded. See "Report on Fidel Castro's Speech on the Twenty-Fifth Anniversary," pp. 10–11. In between these two statements Castro explained that many workers on temporary lay-off were reluctant to go elsewhere for work, because they were receiving 70 percent of their salary while not working; see "Cuban Television Broadcasts Key Parts of Fidel's Remarks at Second Central Committee Plenum," *Granma Weekly Review*, 3 August 1986, p. 5. Together, these statements suggest that in Cuba the labor market remained tight, even where a labor surplus existed, because of the high level at which the state guaranteed the livelihood of workers.

29. "Report on Fidel Castro's Speech at the Meeting," p. 2.

30. Ibid., p. 3.

31. Alexis Codina Jiménez, "Los estimulos materiales y morales en el socialismo," *Economía y Desarrollo* 56 (March/April 1980): 60–61.

32. Ibid., p. 61.

33. For Risquet's statement, see "Primer encuentro nacional de organización y normación del trabajo," *Economía y Desarrollo* 11 (May/June 1972): 200. For the 1980s, see Barbara Flores Casamayor, "Breve analisis del sistema salarial, en los marcos de la Reforma General de Salarios," *Economía y Desarrollo* 78 (January/February 1984): 119; María Díaz Corral and Xionmara Vásquez Grau, "Algunas consideraciones para la aplicación de reglamento de normación del trabajo," *Economía y Desarrollo* 85 (March/April 1985): 227; and Fidel Castro, "Main Report," p. 6.

34. Raúl Castro, "Three Speeches Against Bureaucracy," in Michael Taber (ed.), *Fidel Castro Speeches, Vol. 2: Our Power is That of the Working People* (New York: Pathfinder Press, 1983), pp. 295–96. For a later report of similar manipulations, see "Debates on Rectification," p. 3.

35. "Inspección a 85 empresas avileñas," *Granma*, 8 August 1986, p. 1.
36. Raúl García Pelaez, untitled speech at the closing of the II Reunión Nacional de Chequeo y Control de la vinculación del salario a la norma, *Economía y Desarrollo* 36 (July/August 1976): 208.
37. "Report on Fidel Castro's Speech at the Twenty-Fifth Anniversary," p. 10.
38. García Pelaez, pp. 202, 207-8; and Humberto Pérez, "La obtención de la mayor eficiencia posible en el uso de nuestro recursos," *Economía y Desarrollo* 46 (March/April 1978): 188.
39. "Debates on Rectification," p. 3.
40. Kornai, *Economics*, p. 566. In addition to the difference explained in the text, my analysis diverges from Kornai's in several ways: First, I use the term "bureaucratic centralism" to refer to what Kornai calls "paternalism." Second, I distinguish between malign and benign bureaucratic centralism, whereas Kornai does not distinguish the two, and in fact deals solely with the benign type. Third, I use the terms "systemic" and "sociohistorical" factors to refer, respectively, to what Kornai, *Economics*, pp. 62-63, calls "general" and "special" factors. Kornai's terminology is confusing, because the special factors that he alludes to and the sociohistorical ones that I invoke here have existed "generally," that is, at one time or another in most, perhaps all, of the socialist economies that have existed. Fourth, and most important, my analysis differs from Kornai's in its level of abstraction. Kornai theorizes primarily at the higher level of abstraction suitable to his overriding purpose of comparing capitalist and socialist economies; he therefore focuses almost exclusively on systemic factors. In treating the particular case of Cuba, my analysis necessarily operates at a lower level of abstraction; here, special or sociohistorical factors, such as the peculiarities of different categories of economic actors, require discussion.
41. Kornai, *Economics*, p. 62.
42. For one selection of competing ideas in this area, see *Science & Society* 56, no. 1 (Spring 1992), a special issue on "Socialism: Alternative Visions and Models," and the continuing debate in subsequent issues.

43. Raúl Castro, "Three Speeches," p. 291.
44. No more than a hypothetical status can be claimed for this analysis of sociohistorical factors. It is composed of a series of hypotheses that fit my observations in Cuba, and it is supported by much of the data and analysis offered in this book. But verification would require an empirical research project that included both systematic observations and interviews. As every Cuba scholar knows, and as Pérez-Stable, "Politics and *Conciencia*", has most thoroughly discussed, for a variety of reasons it is virtually impossible for a Cuba scholar from the outside to execute such a project there. The inability to verify these hypotheses is regrettable, but hardly worthy of apology. Cuba scholars may hope for improved access, but they cannot refrain until they have it from drawing conclusions, however hypothetical. It is for the community of such scholars to judge whether these conclusions fit and advance our current state of knowledge.

Chapter 7

Rectification Versus Bureaucratic Centralism in the Late 1980s

Cuba's revolutionary leaders criticized various bureaucratic centralist behaviors and other economic difficulties as early as the late 1970s, but they did not seriously attempt to eliminate these problems until the mid-1980s. For a time, the revolutionary leadership viewed many of these problems as part of a process of adjustment to new mechanisms, like the Economic Management and Planning System (SDPE), and therefore as both inevitable and temporary.[1] Cuban leaders also claimed that the hostility of the Reagan administration in Washington distracted them from their economic problems, which appeared less pressing than the need to build up Cuba's defenses.[2] Perhaps most important, the Cuban economy continued to grow vigorously—on average, according to official figures, 6.7 percent per year—in the first half of the 1980s.[3] So long as this was the case, the bureaucratic centralist plague was more easily tolerated.

In the middle of the 1980s, however, Cuba's economic situation turned ominous.[4] By then, the toll of several years of drought, hurricanes, low international sugar prices, and a variety of other external factors over which the Cubans had no control had mounted. Cost per unit of production, which had dropped slightly from 1981 through 1984, had started to rise due to the excessive wage and materials expenditures of enterprises.[5] Growth rates in critical import-substitution and export industries had become sluggish. All of this squeezed Cuba's hard currency balances, and in 1986, for the first time, the country was unable to meet its debt obligations to capitalist bankers and had to dramatically reduce its imports from the capitalist world.

Not only had Cuba's economic problems become severe, but they could no longer be eased with financial assistance from the capitalist or with increased help from the socialist world. After the rise of Mikhail Gorbachev in 1985, the Soviets began voicing their unwillingness to continue covering the increasing costs of Cuba's economic difficulties.[6] As Fidel Castro reiterated many times in the second half of the 1980s, Cubans no longer had any choice but to solve their economic problems themselves. They had to spur exports and cut imports, to produce more and consume less; they had to attempt to increase efficiency and to eliminate the myriad forms of bureaucratic centralism. To these ends, in 1986 the revolutionary leadership launched a major new rectification drive.

Rectifying Incentives

Fidel Castro sounded one of the central themes of this rectification drive in late 1986: "A consciousness, a communist spirit, a revolutionary will and vocation were, are, and always will be a thousand times more powerful than money."[7] While Castro attacked the overuse of market mechanisms and material incentives, he justified the use of political methods and moral incentives in four related ways. First, he noted that material incentives often have perverse results: When surgeons are remunerated according to their number of operations—one of Castro's favorite examples—both their incomes and the number of needless, even harmful, operations are likely to soar.[8] Second, Castro argued that moral incentives are more powerful than material ones for motivating individuals to act unselfishly and in the general interest: A soldier, for example, might lay down his or her life for national dignity but hardly for a few extra pesos.[9] Third, he underscored that overusing material incentives results in extreme inequality of distribution, characteristic of capitalism but unacceptable under socialism.[10] Fourth, Castro damned the overuse of material incentives for encouraging selfishness, greed, and corruption, while undercutting political consciousness and commitment to the general welfare.[11]

Although all of this echoed statements he had made in the late 1960s, Castro was by no means calling for a return to the *fidelista* period, which he and other revolutionary leaders still looked back upon as a period of idealistic illusions.[12] Castro was calling for an incentive system that, as in the late 1960s, compensated for austerity, for insufficient material incentives, with moral incentives; but he also was calling for a system that, according to the principle promulgated in 1973, rewarded "each according to work." Castro suggested that the value of moral incentives and the need to link material incentives to results had been especially forgotten in the early 1980s. It was then, as noted in Chapter 4, that restrictions on some small-scale private enterprise were relaxed; that the General Wage Reform, which stretched the official wage scales and put greater emphasis on bonuses, was promulgated; that the SDPE, riddled with bureaucratic centralist practices, was extended to virtually the whole economy; and that the presumably morally motivated microbrigades for construction were eliminated. The rectification drive targeted each of these areas.

In early 1986, the revolutionary leadership drastically curbed small-scale private enterprise and abolished the free farmers' markets. The latter, which reportedly accounted for only 2 percent of the total value of marketed food in 1986,[13] were abolished because, even after restrictions had been placed on them in 1982, they continued to suffer from corruption and profiteering. The high profits of some farmers kept them from joining the agricultural cooperatives that the revolutionary leadership had been pushing for a decade. In addition, the population deeply resented that some sellers on these markets charged excessively high prices and gained astronomical incomes—annual takes of 100,000 to 300,000 pesos were from time to time mentioned in the Cuban press. As Fidel Castro put it: "The people bought but they felt they had been robbed."[14]

The leadership further cut material incentives in December 1986, when it introduced a moderate austerity program. Among other things, the leadership cut back assignments of state-owned cars, per diem payments to government officials, and foreign travel budgets and increased charges for some parallel market goods, consumer utility use, and public transportation.[15] Partly to relieve the burden of these measures on the lowest-paid workers, Fidel Castro soon called for the bottom of the official wage scales, eighty-five pesos per month, to be raised to 100 pesos.[16] In calling for this increase, Castro criticized the 1980 General Wage Reform as the creation of those "who have nothing in common with the modest worker."[17] Although strict egalitarianism was still not possible in Cuba, he went on to explain, stretching the wage scales too much was intolerable and resembled capitalism; neither extreme fit the socialist principle of "to each according to work."

Castro claimed, in fact, that raising the lowest wages would be financed by savings from better application and enforcement of this principle: work norms (once again) were to be applied properly so that they would no longer lead to overpayment for little or no work. To this end, Communist Party members were mobilized against managers who tried to elicit worker cooperation through the types of bureaucratic central- ist deals discussed in the previous chapter, and party-led commissions were set up to take over the responsibilities of hiring and firing workers to prevent managers from hoarding labor.

In early 1987, Fidel Castro praised the accomplishments of the party in reducing the demand for workers in selected new facilities through properly applying norms. The prospective work force at the new Guanabacoa bathroom fixtures factory, for example, was reduced from 1,900 to 1,100.[18] But the revolutionary leadership recognized that fully correcting the problem of overstaffing would take many years. On the one hand, it acknowledged that many managers continued to resist the proper use of work norms.[19] It was, in fact, probably out of frustration with this and other sorts of resistance that many of the bureaucratic centralist behaviors of managers, which Fidel Castro had first dubbed "mistakes," were later branded "antisocial, criminal activities" and "acts of disloyalty."[20] On the other hand, the revolutionary leadership recognized that, while it could try to establish a workable system of norms for new factories, it could not all at once correct the problems in existing ones without inducing massive unemployment and attendant political problems.[21] The revolutionary leadership foresaw rectification in this area going on for many years.

One way in which the rectification effort reemphasized moral incentives was by reintroducing microbrigades.[22] These brigades, which were first formed in 1971, were made up of workers who volunteered to temporarily leave their regular jobs and to construct housing and other facilities for their fellow workers and for the society as a whole. Because enter- prises had to pay the salaries of their workers who volunteered for microbrigades, they were considered incompatible with the requirement that SDPE enterprises realize a profit, and fell into disuse after 1980. In 1986, the revolutionary leadership solved this problem by having the state reimburse enterprises for the salaries of their absent volunteers. The microbrigade movement was further expanded in 1988 with the introduction of so-called social brigades, largely made up not of regularly employed workers but of housewives, youths between school and job, and other available community residents.

The revolutionary leadership also stressed moral incentives by exhorting everyone to raise their revolutionary consciousness and to let the general social interest guide their behavior. In addition, it called on administrative personnel not to try to buy the cooperation of others with material incentives but to engage in political work. This did not mean, as Fidel Castro underscored,[23] that administrative personnel were to merely mouth slogans and passages from Marx and Lenin, as had old cadre chatterers in the past. It meant instead that administrators were to strike a good example in their own behavior and also attempt to motivate others by appealing to their political consciousness.

Rectifying Economic Management and Workers' Participation

The rectification drive launched in 1986 was preceded by and included changes in both macroeconomic and microeconomic management. At the same time as these changes further centralized control over the macroeconomy under the top revolutionary leadership, they decentralized responsibility for the microeconomy. These changes sought to turn enterprises into semiautonomous units, such as were envisioned but never realized in the past, with new professional managers capable of making and taking responsibility for an increasing number of decisions and willing to encourage effective workers' participation.

In late 1984, Fidel Castro criticized new professional "technocrats" at the Central Planning Board (JUCEPLAN) for failing to limit the demands of the different ministries in the interests of the national economy, and Cuba's top leaders, organized in a newly created Central Group (*Grupo Estatal Central*), centralized many of JUCEPLAN's former functions in their own hands.[24] In 1986, Fidel Castro announced a hardening of the budget and price constraints on enterprises: it was decreed that unprofitable enterprises, which one estimate put at over one-third of all the enterprises in the country, would no longer automatically be bailed out by the National Bank.[25] In the same year, the revolutionary leadership set up a national commission to study the many problems of the SDPE and to propose solutions based on Cuba's situation and experiences. Such studies soon resulted in a proliferation of experiments in Cuban enterprises and work centers.

One set of experiments was known as the Revolutionary Armed Forces Initiative.[26] This began at the military's Che Guevara Industrial Complex in 1987, and, because of its effectiveness in reducing costs and increasing output, was applied to all military enterprises in 1989 and to an increasing number of civilian enterprises beginning in 1990. This multifaceted initiative involved, among other things, reorganizing work, upping norms, and laying off excess personnel. It eliminated promotion by seniority, which benefited old cadres over new professionals; introduced various management techniques—quality control circles, management by consensus, participatory decision-making, etc.—derived from capitalist corporations; as well as devolving more control to managers, while encouraging them to solve problems without waiting for orders from above. Further, it reduced central directives to enterprises, which now would become semiautonomous units.

Another set of experiments that the Cubans ardently publicized were their work contingents in the construction industry. These were first introduced with the formation of the Blas Roca Contingent in October 1987.[27] By 1989, Cuba had sixty-two such contingents with over 30,000 workers, all chosen from a pool of volunteers.

Those chosen are generally young—90 percent of workers in the Blas Roca Contingent, for example, were less than thirty years of age in 1992—and capable of working up to fifteen hours per day (an extreme, scheduled to be reduced in the future). In return for such lengthy labor, contingent members receive an expanded diet, intensive medical monitoring, special attention to their personal or familial needs, etc; and they get paid—in accord with their greater amount of work—more than other workers at their level. In 1989, for example, contingent members produced 130 to 200 percent more in value and were paid from 25 to 50 percent more than the average construction worker. Still, moral incentives are showered on contingent members: they are regularly held up as heroes to their neighbors and to the nation.

The contingents are designed to be both lean in administration and rich in participation. Contingents operate with one-half to one-third of the proportion of nonmanual personnel used in other production units, and contingent managers and technicians are expected to work on-site and to callous their hands.

In the contingents, groups of workers are given equipment, supplies, and full, start-to-finish, responsibility for a particular project. These groups kick off each day with a collective review of their previous day's efforts. They discuss the quantity, quality, and the cost of what was produced, and the performance of themselves as a group and as individual workers; and they review their plans for the day ahead.

Popular and workers' participation was a focus of attention ever since the revolutionary leadership launched its rectification drive in 1986. The leadership never viewed rectifying Cuba's economic problems as solely a high-level affair; it recognized that many problems could be solved only with greater popular participation. As a result, the revolutionary leadership mobilized workers through their trade unions and under the direction of the party to seek solutions to economic problems and to expose the administrative personnel partially responsible for them. Although rejecting the desirability of a "cultural revolution" that would "throw the people against those responsible," Fidel Castro called on workers to help the party find solutions in an "organized and disciplined manner."[28]

Beginning in 1986, workers and the wider population became directly involved in various efforts to rectify Cuba's economic practices. During that year, for example, the party program, which, among other things, detailed the operating principles of the SDPE, was submitted to the population for discussion. In the process, people not only were able to criticize the operation of the SDPE in Cuba, but also to deepen their overall understanding of the country's economic problems. Later, Fidel Castro called for worker and trade union participation in uncovering why so many enterprises, even many that were well-run, failed to realize a profit.[29]

The Cuban leadership also began to address some of the problems mentioned in the last chapter with workers' participation. In 1986, for example, after the revolutionary leadership had underscored that workers needed information if they were to participate effectively, it was announced that planning authorities had delivered the requisite figures to all enterprises, perhaps for the first time ever, early enough for workers to discuss them.[30]

In 1988, the leadership began introducing a system of "continuous planning." Prior to this, managers and workers had typically discussed the plan for their area only after it had been fully formulated (and delivered) by higher authorities. Now managers and workers were not to wait: they were to take the initiative by elaborating their own plan first, and to negotiate their differences with higher authorities afterwards. During 1988, continuous planning was tested in thirty-two enterprises, and by 1990 it had been extended to some 900 enterprises, responsible for 48 percent of the Cuba's mercantile production and employing 38 percent of its productive sector workers.[31]

Rectifying Intermediate-level Personnel

Although the rectification drive launched in 1986 reasserted the importance of popular and workers' participation, the revolutionary leadership had not overlooked that workers previously participated in a variety of negative economic practices. But Cuban leaders publicly blamed these behaviors less on workers than on the administrative personnel involved. As Fidel Castro declared in mid-1986: "The workers are not to blame for this. The guilty ones are the leadership personnel, the administrative personnel."[32]

Further reforming Cuba's intermediate-level personnel was, in fact, a central element of the rectification effort. On the one hand, in 1986 Fidel Castro both attacked the General Wage Reform of 1980 for inordinately benefiting these personnel and reiterated his earlier criticisms of new professionals who had attempted to materially exploit their educational advantages. On the other hand, just as Cuban leaders blamed serious economic errors on Humberto Pérez and his fellow "technocrats" at JUCEPLAN in late 1984, so they continued to blame certain new professionals for economic problems in 1986. Fidel Castro, for example, criticized managers who had tried to buy workers' cooperation with money. He castigated administrators who had tried to solve problems by increasing prices, for example, "technocrats" who had attempted to build up the railroads by raising prices on highway transport, when they could have simply ordered certain agencies to increase their rail use.[33] In fact, Castro blamed a host of economic problems on the enthusiasm of "technocrats" for "capitalist" methods.[34]

Such criticisms, however, should not be taken as evidence that the revolutionary leadership did not "appear to hold the training and skills" of the new professional stratum "in high regard."[35] For one thing, these criticisms targeted, not the whole new professional stratum, but only individuals and tendencies within the stratum. For another, the rectification drive targeted not just certain new professionals but the old cadres as well. In fact, the thrust of the rectification effort begun in 1986 was to hasten rather than to impede the transition from old cadres to new professionals.

This is clear, first of all, from the statements of Fidel Castro in this period. During and after 1986, Castro continued to attack old cadre administrators who, out of buddyism and fear for their jobs, had protected their own kind and held back the young new professionals under them.[36] He also called for something that, as seen above, was eventually realized under the Revolutionary Armed Forces Initiative: he demanded that educational credentials, not seniority, which of course benefited the old cadres, be used to determine who remained and who rose in intermediate-level positions.[37] Furthermore, while damning the technocratic propensities of some new professionals, Fidel Castro continued to call for intermediate-level personnel who had "master[ed] the science of organization and management."[38] And he touted the need for trained economic professionals to make detailed analyses of the operation of Cuba's economic mechanisms and to assist the revolutionary leadership in correcting the country's economic problems.[39]

But the conclusion that the 1986 rectification effort aimed to speed the changeover from old cadres to new professionals rests on more than the statements of Cuba's preeminent revolutionary leader. The Communist Party's Third Congress, held in 1986, reaffirmed the personnel policy for training, selecting, evaluating, and promoting members of the administrative apparatus that, as described in Chapter 5, the Communist Party had first promulgated in 1975.[40] A national working group, charged by the party in August 1986 to investigate the effectiveness of this policy, however, found that it had not been widely or consistently implemented; and in February 1988, a commission, linked to the Council of Ministers, was set up to rectify the matter. In its 1988 year-end report, the party's working group underscored that poor managerial performance strongly correlated with managers' higher age and lower educational level, and that a large number of intermediate-level positions—especially, as noted in Chapter 5, managerial positions in older areas of the economy—had been retained by undereducated old cadres.

The party's working group also criticized practices that ensured managers' job security regardless of performance, lifetime retention of positions, and promotion based on seniority, each of which, of course, benefited old cadres at the expense of new professionals. It was further noted that old cadre managers often had found it difficult to communicate with the younger and more highly educated new professionals, and that old cadre managers often had failed to cultivate, or even discriminated against, the new professionals below them. The underutilization of new professionals was pointed out by a study of the Nicaro nickel plant, which revealed that, of its 184 engineers, only 6 percent were utilized in "a satisfactory manner," 70 percent were "underutilized," and the rest were used "poorly."[41]

The party's working group also recognized that some measure of discrimination against new professionals was more specifically aimed against women. The majority of both old cadre and new professional managers are men, but a sizeable and growing proportion of younger new professionals, as seen in Chapter 5, are women. Although Cuban women have advanced dramatically under the revolution, they still suffer from various types of discrimination.[42] This is true for Cuban women in general and for Cuba's young new professional women in particular. It was for this reason that in 1989 the party's working group came out strongly against the scarcity of women managers. It noted that, since women made up over half of Cuba's economic and management specialists, plenty of women stood ready to move into managerial positions. These women, the working group recommended, should be advanced immediately.[43]

By December 1986, more than 400 administrators in Havana, including 120 enterprise and work center managers, had been removed from their posts, as had eighty-five grassroots party leaders, because of their unwillingness or inability to change their behavior;[44] and this was just the beginning of a drive that continues to this day to shake up and reduce the size of Cuba's administrative apparatus. Although this drive has ejected some new professionals from administrative posts, the majority of those demoted or removed doubtless have been old cadres. It seems clear that in 1986 the revolutionary leadership changed its formerly gradualist policy and sped up the transition from old cadres to new professionals in administrative positions.

Even though Cuba's real economic growth sputtered in the

final years of the 1980s—from 1986 to 1989, gross social product (GSP) grew at an average annual rate of only .38 percent, and GSP per capita dropped at an average annual rate of .65 percent[45]—Cuban leaders consistently praised the rectification drive. They extolled the rectification drive for its positive effects overall, especially for raising the general level of political consciousness about the need to consume less and to produce more with greater efficiency and for mitigating various forms of bureaucratic centralism, and for its concrete accomplishments in particular areas.

Havana's microbrigades, for example, were applauded for having built 16,515 apartments and 111 childcare centers, as well as many other facilities; and, nationally, for having helped to expand twenty-four hospitals and to build nine new hospitals, twenty-seven community health clinics, 6,500 home-office complexes for family doctors and nurses, 324 childcare centers, 154 schools, and tens of thousands of apartments, etc.[46] Construction contingents were hailed for rapidly finishing, at dramatically reduced costs, increased numbers of highways and bridges, irrigation systems and reservoirs, tourist hotels and resorts, as well as many other kinds of projects.[47] And the Revolutionary Armed Forces Initiative in its first two years at the military's Che Guevara Industrial Complex was commended for reportedly having brought about a fifteen-cent cost reduction per unit of production (leading to a considerable saving overall), a 10 percent cut in personnel, a 2.4 percent increase in salaries, a 69 percent increase in production, as well as improvements in quality.[48]

Regardless of how the immediate effects of the rectification process are evaluated, however, Cuban leaders never intended this process to be judged solely by its short term results. They envisioned that rectification would go on for many years. In 1989, however, after only about three years of rectification,

Cuba's effort was dramatically intruded upon by the beginning of the collapse of Soviet-bloc Communism. Cuba's revolutionary leaders would continue to pursue various rectification measures, but they would now have to add other measures designed solely to enhance the survival chances of the revolution, as it plunged into its worst crisis ever.

Notes

1. "Report on Fidel Castro's Closing Remarks at the 53rd Plenary of the National Council of the Central Organization of Cuban Trade Unions," *Granma Weekly Review,* 1 February 1987, pp. 2–4.
2. Ibid.
3. This figure is for gross social product from 1980 to 1985, as reported by Andrew Zimbalist, "Cuban Political Economy and Cubanology: An Overview," in his edited volume *Cuban Political Economy: Controversies in Cubanology* (Boulder, CO: Westview Press, 1988), p. 2. For an excellent review of the controversy over Cuba's official statistics and economic performance, see Andrew Zimbalist and Claes Brundenius, *The Cuban Economy: Measurement and Analysis of Socialist Performance* (Baltimore: The Johns Hopkins University Press, 1989).
4. For a brief overview of Cuba's economic problems, see Fidel Castro, "Speech to the 3rd Congress of the Committees for the Defense of the Revolution," *Granma Weekly Review,* 12 October 1986, p. 3.
5. See the remarks of José M. Acosta, "Meeting of Basic Industry Enterprise Directors," *Granma Weekly Review,* 15 February 1987, pp. 4–5.
6. See "Report on Fidel Castro's Closing Remarks at the Meeting of the Provincial Committee of the Party," *Granma Weekly Review,* 25 January 1987, p. 2.
7. "Report on Fidel Castro's Closing Remarks at the 53rd Plenary," p. 2; and his remarks in "Debates on Rectification of Errors and Negative Tendencies in Various Spheres of Society at the

Deferred Session of the Third Congress of the Communist Party of Cuba," *Granma Weekly Review*, 4 December 1986, p. 2.

8. "Report on Fidel Castro's Closing Remarks at the 53rd Plenary," p. 4.

9. Fidel Castro, "Speech to the Third Congress," *Granma Weekly Review*, 12 October 1986, p. 4.

10. "Report on Fidel Castro's Closing Remarks at the 53rd Plenary," p. 2.

11. "Report on Fidel Castro's Closing Remarks at the Meeting of the Provincial Committee," p. 2.

12. "Report on Fidel Castro's Closing Remarks at the 53rd Plenary," p. 2.

13. Fidel Castro, "Closing Speech at the Second National Meeting of Agricultural Production Cooperatives," *Granma Weekly Review*, 1 June 1986, pp. 3-4.

14. Ibid.

15. "Report on Fidel Castro's Analysis of the Economic Situation and the Essential Measures to Be Taken," *Granma Weekly Review*, 11 January 1987, pp. 2-5.

16. "Report on Fidel Castro's Closing Remarks at the 53rd Plenary," p. 4.

17. Ibid., p. 2.

18. "Report on Fidel Castro's Closing Remarks at the Provincial Committee," p. 4.

19. "Report on Fidel Castro's Closing Remarks at the 53rd Plenary," p. 4.

20. Ibid., p. 2.

21. Fidel Castro, "Speech to the Third Congress," p. 4; "Report on Fidel Castro's Analysis of the Economic Situation," p. 4.

22. "Report on Fidel Castro's Speech at the Opening of the Julio Trigo Hospital," *Granma Weekly Review*, 20 September 1987, p. 4.

23. Fidel Castro, "Speech at the Close of the Deferred Session of the Third Congress of the Communist Party of Cuba," *Granma Weekly Review*, 14 December 1986, p. 13.

24. *Granma Weekly Review*, 29 December 1984; 4 January 1985; 11 February 1985. In 1988, these functions were shifted to the Executive Committee of the Council of Ministers.

25. "National Meeting of Party's Economic Departments," *Granma Weekly Review,* 15 February 1987, p. 1.
26. Marc Frank, *Cuba Looks to the Year 2,000* (New York: International Publishers, 1993), pp. 51-55; and Andrew Zimbalist, "Teetering on the Brink: Cuba's Current Economic and Political Crisis," *Journal of Latin American Studies* 24: 407-418.
27. The following information is from Ulises Estrada Lescaille, "Con espíritu de contingente," *Granma International,* 12 June 1992, p. 11; and Frank, pp. 44-51.
28. "Report on Fidel Castro's Speech at the 25th Anniversary of the Proclamation of the Socialist Nature of the Revolution and the Victory at Playa Girón," *Granma Weekly Review,* 27 April 1986, p. 10.
29. "Report on Fidel Castro's Closing Remarks at the 53rd Plenary Meeting," p. 4.
30. José A. López Moreno, "Report on the Fulfillment of the 1985 Plan for Economic and Social Development and the Objectives Set for 1986," *Granma Weekly Review,* 12 January 1986, p. 4.
31. Frank, pp. 57-61.
32. Fidel Castro, "Closing Speech at the Second National Meeting," p. 4.
33. *Granma Weekly Review,* 6 July 1986, p. 2.
34. Ibid.
35. Rhoda Rabkin, *Cuban Politics: The Revolutionary Experiment* (New York: Praeger, 1991), p. 74.
36. "Fifth Congress of the Communist Youth League (UJC)," *Granma Weekly Review,* 12 April 1987, p. 5; and see also the "Deferred Session of the Fifth Central Committee Plenum," *Granma Weekly Review,* 4 October 1987, p. 5.
37. Fidel Castro, "Speech at the Main Ceremony to Commemorate the 35th Anniversary of the Attack on Moncada," *Granma Weekly Review,* 7 August 1988, pp. 2-5.
38. "Report on Fidel Castro's Remarks at the Second Meeting of Havana Enterprises," *Granma Weekly Review,* 5 July 1987, p. 5.
39. Ibid.
40. Unless otherwise noted, the following information on personnel policy is gathered from Frank, pp. 61-65.

41. "Meeting of the Enterprise Directors of the Ministry of Basic Industry," *Granma Weekly Review,* 7 August 1988, pp. 2-5.

42. See the excellent discussion by Carollee Bengelsdorf, "On the Problem of Studying Women in Cuba," in Zimbalist, ed., *Cuban Political Economy,* pp. 119-36; also of interest are Vilma Espin, *Cuban Women Confront the Future* (Melbourne, Australia: Ocean Press, and New York: Center for Cuban Studies, 1992); and Margaret Randall, *Gathering Rage: The Failure of 20th Century Revolutions to Develop a Feminist Agenda* (New York: Monthly Review Press, 1992).

43. Frank, p. 65.

44. "Debates on Rectification of Errors," pp. 8-9.

45. Author's computations from *The Economist* Intelligence Unit, *Cuba: Country Profile, 1992-93* (London: The Economist, Fourth Quarter 1993), p. 12.

46. See Frank, pp. 81-83.

47. Ibid., pp. 49-51.

48. Ibid., p. 51.

Chapter 8

Conclusion:
The "Special Period" Crisis

Two sets of factors accounted for the severity of the crisis that Cuba began to enter at the end of 1989. One was the rapid disintegration of the Soviet bloc's common market, the Council for Mutual Economic Assistance (CMEA), on which Cuba's economy had become highly dependent. As mentioned before, Cuba joined the CMEA in 1972, started coordinating its five-year economic plans with the CMEA countries in 1976, and, partly in response to very beneficial terms of trade, increasingly concentrated its trade with these countries until 1989.

The other set of factors was revolutionary Cuba's problematic relationship to the capitalist world economy. There, Cuba suffered from worsening terms of trade; and, in 1986, when Cuba stopped paying its capitalist foreign debt—typically estimated at between $6 and $7 million—Cuba became ineligible for anything other than short-term credits. The U.S. blockade, which became even more stringent with the passage of the misnamed Cuban Democracy Act in 1992, also hurt Cuba's dealings in the capitalist world economy.[1] As Soviet-bloc Communism collapsed and the U.S. blockade tightened, the Cubans found themselves confronting what they have sometimes called a "double blockade."

The Economic Crisis Unfolds

The first economic ripples from the Soviet-bloc collapse hit Cuban shores in January 1990, when CMEA shipments of wheat, grains, and other materials for livestock feed and bread had already started to lag. By September, Fidel Castro declared that Cuba had entered a "special period in time of peace," but the full impact of the Soviet-bloc collapse had not yet struck the island. Cuban trade with Eastern European countries fell by about half in 1990 and all but disappeared in 1991, but Cuban trade with the Soviet Union fell much less drastically. In 1990, as calculated in rubles, Cuban exports to the Soviet Union declined only 9.6 percent and Soviet exports to Cuba dipped by a significant but not drastic 13.2 percent.[2] In the last days of 1990, Fidel Castro could still say that, although everyone had to be ready for Cuba's situation to worsen, it was still "not very acute, [not] very serious."[3]

On December 30, 1990, when Cuban and Soviet negotiators finally announced their agreement on the following year's economic accord, it was revealed that the two countries had scrapped all five-year commitments for a one-year arrangement.[4] Pricing was now to be in hard currency at world market levels; the only exception was the price of sugar, which, although reduced from the 1990 price of $800 per ton to $500 per ton, was maintained above the world market price. Each country vowed to supply goods and services valued at about $5 billion, and the Soviets pledged to deliver 10 million tons of oil, down from the 13 million tons supplied annually in the early 1980s. Although $1 billion in Soviet aid was to be carried over from earlier agreements, the 1991 agreement included no new development aid for Cuba.

The 1991 accord necessitated more belt-tightening in Cuba. Imports had to be pared to essentials, such as fuel, food, and critical raw materials. With fuel and electricity tightly rationed, it no longer made sense to distribute household appliances and cars, and such imports were eliminated altogether. Due to lack of fuel, even imports of tractors and trucks for agricultural production were cut to the minimum. The 1991 agreement contained a Soviet promise not to reduce food deliveries to Cuba, but this promise, like many others, would not be kept.

On October 10, 1991, in his opening address to the Fourth Congress of the Cuban Communist Party, Fidel Castro lamented the deterioration of Cuban-Soviet trade.[5] He explained that, up to the end of September, the Soviets had delivered all the fuel but only 26 percent of the total goods that they had promised. Almost no foodstuffs had arrived in the first five months of the year, and deliveries still had not caught up by the end of September: Cuba had received only half of the promised split peas, 7 percent of the lard, 16 percent of the vegetable oil, 11 percent of the condensed milk, 47 percent of the butter, 18 percent of the canned meat, 22 percent of the powdered milk, 11 percent of fresh and canned fish.

Soviet deliveries of important household items were also far behind: By the end of September, Cuba had received no detergent, less than 5 percent of the expected soap, and just over 1 percent of the spare parts for Soviet-made television sets and refrigerators. The Cuban-Soviet agreement had drastically reduced planned deliveries of agricultural, construction, and transportation equipment, but actual deliveries fell even further: By the end of September, Cuba had received only 38 percent of the equipment and only 10 percent of the spare parts that the Soviets had pledged to supply in this category. At the same time, Cuba had received only 16 percent of the fertilizers promised by the Soviets, none of the wood pulp for paper, 2 percent of the paper and cardboard, 1.6 percent of the tires, 15 percent of the tin, 1.9 percent of the laminated steel—and the list went on.

But the worst was yet to come. The faltering deliveries of 1991 reflected not only the Soviet Union's economic problems but also its political conflicts. These latter came to a head in August 1991 when an aborted coup paved the way for the fall of Mikhail Gorbachev, the demise of the Soviet Communist Party, and the breakup of the Soviet Union, all of which threatened Cuba with even worse economic straits. In 1992, Cuba's total trade with its former CMEA allies dropped to only 7 percent of what it had been in 1989; also in 1992, Cuba imported from Russia only 1.8 million tons of oil, a mere 13.5 percent of what it had imported from the Soviet Union in 1989.[6]

Not until 1993, however, did Cuba face the full and combined force of the collapse of Soviet-bloc Communism and of the U.S. economic blockade, newly strengthened by the malicious Cuban Democracy Act. In 1993, primarily because of this "double blockade" and particularly destructive weather conditions, Cuban sugar production, which had averaged 7.5 million tons per year in the period from 1987 to 1991, dropped to a low 4.2 million tons. The country braced to earn hard currency sufficient to pay for little more than its planned imports of food and fuel; and the value of Cuba's total imports fell another 24 percent.[7] By 1993, the Cuban revolution had entered the full depths of crisis.

The Economic Response

Cuba's leaders attempted to ensure the revolution's survival by responding to this crisis immediately. Facing precipitously declining aid, imports, and markets, at the beginning of the crisis the leadership introduced a series of measures, which, as the crisis deepened, it intensified and expanded. The leadership tried with varying success to, among other things, maintain and, in some cases, even increase exports, especially to hard currency areas; provide consumers and industry with at least minimal supplies of essential inputs, especially energy; sustain the population's basic subsistence, especially its food supply; and continue to provide free, universal, and effective social security, health, and educational services.

In pursuit of such ends, the revolutionary leadership has been willing to bend established political principles—but only so far. They have recognized that they can no longer continue to "build" socialism during the special period. But they have remained committed to preserving socialism's achievements,[8] including the free and universal services just mentioned and as much collective control of the economy as possible. Cuba's leaders, unlike many former Soviet-bloc leaders, have neither embraced capitalism or neoliberalism nor renounced socialism, but they have responded to the crisis pragmatically.

Cuba's leaders have not, for example, entertained a wholesale sell-off of state property to foreign investors—or any sell-off to Cuban citizens—but since the outbreak of the current crisis they have opened to foreign investors far wider than ever before. Cuba recently amended its Constitution and liberalized its foreign investment regulations, which had been on the books since 1982, to offer, among other things, unrestricted profit repatriation, generous tax holidays, and investment security. Even though the U.S. government has been trying to scare off Cuba's potential partners, by March 1994 Cuban enterprises and foreign investors had entered into 129 economic associations and were discussing many times more.[9] Some of these are cooperative production arrangements, with foreign companies receiving a share of revenues in return for such things as finance, materials, technology, or markets; most are joint ventures, usually involving minority (but in at least one case, majority) foreign ownership. In every case, the Cuban state retains the option not to renew these contracts when they lapse in ten to twenty-five years and to buy out their foreign partners at market value.

This opening to foreign investment, even though selective rather than wholesale, has widened as Cuba's crisis has deepened. Initially, at the outbreak of the crisis, Cuba was interested, perhaps exclusively, in joint ventures that provided it with new facilities. As they entered the full depths of the crisis in 1993, however, Cuba's leaders became willing to sell half-interest in existing facilities, starved for raw materials or markets, in severely depressed industries that had been totally or almost totally closed down. The foreign partner would provide materials and markets, and Cuba would reap, among other things, hard currency. This further opening was made reluctantly but justified pragmatically. As Carlos Lage, a new professional who has risen to become Secretary of Cuba's Council of Ministers, explained: "Look, I know, it's a shock. We wouldn't do it if we were able to run that industry with our own resources, but it's logical given the circumstances we find ourselves in."[10]

Since early in the crisis, the Cuban leadership has sought foreign investments in a broad range of economic areas, including agriculture, fertilizers, pesticides, fishing, textiles, pharmaceuticals, steel, construction materials, food processing, paper, sugar derivatives, and mining. But the island's strongest magnet for attracting foreign investments has been tourism. As of November 1993, over one-fifth and the most important of Cuba's economic associations with foreign capital were in this sector. Cuba's leaders decided to expand tourism before the current crisis, but it was the crisis that forced them to rely so heavily on foreign investments to rapidly expand tourism after 1989. The number of tourists in Cuba grew from 243,026 in 1985 to about 480,000 in 1992; and the Cubans, realistically or not, hope for 1 million tourists in 1995 and 5 to 6 million eventually.[11] To discourage prostitution and other common corruptions of tourism, the Cuban industry first expanded into specialized market niches, such as health and ecology tourism, and initially limited its joint ventures to self-contained resorts, complete with hotels, recreation, and international travel facilities, located in remote, sometimes off-shore, areas. But the industry began to expand in major population centers as the crisis deepened and the need for hard currency increased.

The leadership has also sought foreign investors to expand and improve the Cuban nickel industry. Not only does Cuba possess more than one-third of the world's known nickel reserves, but, because the island's deposits are mostly near the surface and accessible to relatively cheap open-pit technology, the industry could be a big earner of hard currency. In 1991, it was announced that an unnamed Western mining company had invested a sizeable $1.2 billion to increase the quality and quantity of Cuban nickel production. With better quality, Cuban nickel could compete in 40 percent of the world market that previously was out of its reach. By sometime in the second half of the 1990s, moreover, Cuba's leaders hope to have doubled the country's total nickel output.[12]

The Cuban leadership has also looked for foreign investments to help expand the island's newest exports. The most dramatic example is biotechnology, where Cuba rapidly has become a major innovator.[13] Cuba's new professional scientists have genetically engineered and marketed over 200 medical and agricultural products. Some of the medical products are unique in their categories, such as natural and recombinant interferons for treating cancer, AIDS, leprosy, hepatitis C, and schizophrenia; a human transfer factor to boost the immune system; a recombinant streptokinase for rapid dissolution of blood clots after heart attack; an epidermal growth factor for skin regeneration; a hepatitis-B vaccine; the world's first meningitis-B vaccine. The agricultural products include biofertilizers, biobactericides, biopesticides, new plant strains, and cloned seedlings.

Cuba's biotechnology research is geared to both domestic needs and the world market. Before Cuba began to sell its meningitis-B vaccine to other third world countries, for example, it became the first (and still only) country to vaccinate all of its newborns; and Cuba has been using biotechnology products for import substitution and increased productivity in agriculture. Cuba's ability to turn its biotechnology industry into a major hard currency earner, however, is uncertain. Thus, to expand its mass production capabilities and to further break into world markets that are restricted by the U.S. blockade and dominated by transnational monopolies, Cuba has entered into associations with foreign capital.[14]

One of the top priority areas where Cuba's revolutionary leaders have solicited foreign investors has been in the production of energy, especially petroleum. As already seen, beginning in the second half of the 1970s Cuba entered into a very favorable sugar-for-oil deal with the Soviet Union. By the late 1980s, Cuba depended on oil for almost three-quarters of its energy needs and on the Soviet Union for 90 to 95 percent of its petroleum supply. But the sugar-for-oil deal was not renewed and the amount of oil that Cuba received from the Soviet, and, then, formerly Soviet, republics subsequently plummeted. Short on hard currency and locked in by the U.S. blockade, moreover, Cuba had difficulty making arrangements with new suppliers and slipped into a severe energy crisis.[15]

Here the revolutionary leadership first responded with extensive and deep cutbacks. Beginning in 1990, the leadership slashed gasoline supplies for private and government vehicles; pared bus and train schedules to the bone; eliminated nighttime sporting events; curtailed television transmissions to a few hours a day; reduced electricity supplies to offices, factories, farms, and homes during peak hours; instituted rolling blackouts in Havana; and shut down means of production, including fleets of tractors and whole factories. To cushion the impact of some of this, Cuban leaders decided to import bicycles from China and to begin producing bicycles domestically. They also significantly increased the use of oxen for agriculture and of other draft animals for transporting people and goods. Cuba even opened a new post office for deliveries between Havana and the provinces by carrier pigeon.

The shortage has challenged Cuba's leaders to search for new domestic energy sources. On the one hand, they have sought non-petroleum sources; on the other, they have pushed to dramatically increase the domestic production of petroleum.

The new professionals at Cuba's National Energy Commission have estimated that non-petroleum energy could one day supply the country with the equivalent of 8 million tons of petroleum.[15] The Cubans experimented with burning wood in locomotives; cultivated fast-growing plant varieties for fuel; used increasing amounts of bagasse (a sugar by-product) to power sugar mills; and developed more hydroelectric, biogas, and solar sources. Meanwhile, they continued work on their Juraguá nuclear plant. By March 1992, after a hiatus that put the whole project in question, Russia had agreed to take up where the Soviet Union left off in supplying technical advice and materials, and West European companies had begun negotiating with the Cubans to supply other elements to complete the project. Although behind schedule, Cuba's only nuclear plant, originally slated to start up in 1987, could go on line by 1995.[17]

Before the revolution, Cuba had produced no more than 120,000 tons of petroleum in any year; in 1993, however, Cuba produced over 1 million tons, and much of the increase was due to recent initiatives. According to Marcos Portal, Cuba's Minister of Basic Industry, since 1989 the island has doubled or quadrupled the output of some its existing wells simply by shifting from Soviet to Western technology.[17] Moreover, even before 1993, when Cuba held its first international auction of oil exploration and production concessions, both European and Latin American companies had started to invest in the expanding oil production on the island.[19]

At the very beginning of the current crisis, Cuba's leaders declared that their top economic priority was maintaining the country's food supply. So in December 1989, the leadership announced a major food program (*Programa Alimentario– PA*),[20] with several objectives. First, the PA pressed to decrease dependence on imported food. Over the course of the revolution, Cuba's dependence on food imports had lessened, dropping from 20 percent of total imports in 1970 to less than 10 percent in the second half of the 1980s. Still, Cuba had to import high proportions of certain foods. Wheat and wheat flour, for example, which could not be grown in Cuba, were totally imported, mostly from the Soviet Union. When Soviet deliveries of wheat started to slip in 1990, Cuba's leaders immediately cut back bread rations and, in Havana, raised bread prices; but by the end of the 1990, they were stepping up research into making bread with tropical products (cassava, sweet potato, sorghum) instead of imported wheat.[21] The PA also sought to increase the domestic production of rice and of other food-stuffs that Cuba both grew and imported.

The PA's second objective was to increase the availability of meat, dairy, poultry, fruit, and vegetable products by improving distribution through increasing storage capacity and speeding deliveries and by increasing output through expanding irrigation, production facilities, and acreage. Although some land was taken out of sugar production to grow foodstuffs, the PA sought to maintain sugar output by increasing yields. Sugar was slated not only to remain the country's major hard currency earner for years to come, but also to remain an important source of animal feed and of inputs for a variety of industries.

Third, the PA sought to increase local and regional agricultural production to economize on resources, especially energy, and to utilize available labor power. Beginning in 1990, seeds and gardening manuals were distributed to homes and work centers so that they could turn their yards, patios, and roofs into what one observer likened to the "victory gardens" cultivated in the United States during World War II.[22] The almost 800,000 Cuban gardens that had come into existence by the end of 1991 not only supplemented family meals but also saved transportation resources and freed up state food supplies for hospitals, schools, etc.

The PA also sought to ensure the food supply for Cuba's largest urban area and to save energy on transportation by making the city and province of Havana self-sufficient in certain types of food, especially vegetables and root crops. Here, however, the PA came up against a chronic shortage of agricultural labor. This shortage first appeared early in the revolution, when expanding opportunities for education and employment in urban areas began to lure workers out of agriculture.

Over the course of the revolution, the revolutionary leadership compensated for scarce agricultural labor with periodic mobilizations of urban dwellers—university students, new professionals, manual workers, housewives, political leaders, etc.—but especially with large-scale agricultural mechanization, requiring increased amounts of both fertilizer and fuel. As these latter became less available during the special period, the revolutionary leadership again called on urbanites to work in agriculture for two to three week stints.

The leadership also introduced agricultural work contingents. These were modeled on the construction contingents discussed in the last chapter, and comprised of urban volunteers willing to make a two year commitment. As the revolution's crises deepened and increasing numbers of work centers closed for lack of resources, members of contingents and unemployed urban workers were encouraged, with promises of new housing and other facilities, to resettle in the countryside and to transfer to agricultural work permanently.

It became obvious by 1993 that the PA and related efforts were insufficient to reverse the deterioration of food and agricultural production in Cuba. In that year the "double blockade" combined with particularly devastating weather to produce the lowest sugar output, 4.2 million tons, since the early days of the revolution, along with worsening food shortages. By then, caring relatives and friends in Miami were sending food baskets valued at $235 million per year;[23] but while these supplemented the diet of some Cubans sometimes, overall they simply called attention to the revolution's crisis.

This crisis was further underscored with the diagnosis, from late 1992 to September 1993, of over 50,000 cases of a mysterious nerve and vision disorder, caused in part by dietary deficiencies. This epidemic was quickly brought under control when daily vitamin pills were distributed free to the entire population, but the revolution's food and agricultural problems remained.[24] At the same time, declining resources were making it harder to resolve Cuba's agricultural labor shortage. Short-term mobilizations for agricultural work became more difficult, as the revolution's rural housing programs, and subsequently the resettlement of urban dwellers to the countryside, faltered.

At least partly in response, in September 1993 the revolutionary leadership officially announced a dramatic agricultural reform that turned state farms into cooperatives. Similar changes had been underway for some time, but only in selected areas; now, not all, but over half of the state farmland across the country is being parcelled out to groups of workers organized into Basic Units of Cooperative Production (*Unidades Básicas de Producción Cooperativa*–UBPC).[25]

The UBPCs do not own land, but they do have the right to use their parcel of land for an indefinite period. They are extended credit to buy and to insure their equipment and raw materials. They elect their own leaders, organize their own production, and take care of their own financial obligations. The UBPCs are expected to produce their own food and to supply a contracted amount of sugar or other crops to their state farm enterprises, which are empowered to dissolve those UBPCs that fail to follow regulations or to meet their financial or production commitments.

In short, the UBPCs offer workers the right to work state-owned land and the chance for a steady supply of homegrown food and a better standard of living in the hope of spurring resource savings, higher production yields, and rural resettlement. Council of Ministers Secretary Lage predicted that 60 percent of the workers in Havana's agricultural contingents will be willing to move to the countryside and join the UBPCs, and that the latter will increase agricultural output overall and ensure homegrown food for at least 3 million workers and family members.[26] Only time, of course, will tell.

The UBPCs are just a recent example of the continuing economic reforms in Cuba that have decentralized many economic decisions and responsibilities. Some such reforms, like the Revolutionary Armed Forces Initiative discussed in the last chapter, were introduced at the peak of the rectification drive after 1986 and spread even more widely after 1989. Other such reforms seem to have been the product of the "special period" crisis itself. The Ministry of Foreign Trade, for example, has allowed some enterprises to handle their own foreign trade and to retain a large proportion of their hard currency earnings to purchase their own foreign inputs. And other, even more far-reaching, reforms are in the offing. In his address to the National Assembly in December 1993, Cuba's new Minister of Finance (and a new professional) José Luís Rodríguez explained that the state budget deficit had jumped from 1.4 billion pesos in 1989 to 4.1 billion pesos in 1993, largely because the state had been covering the losses of the 69 percent of enterprises that were operating in the red as a result of the country's economic crisis. State subsidies to such enterprises, he stated, would have to be systematically reduced.[27]

Cuba's leaders obviously consider some of the reforms that they have introduced as regrettable but necessary for now— that is, until the end of the "special period" crisis.[28] Among such reforms was the legalization of self-employment. This was approved by the Fourth Party Congress in 1991 but not implemented until September 1993 in recognition of the fact that the state could no longer supply the population with either sufficient services or sufficient employment. This reform legalized self-employment in 117 areas, including masons, locksmiths, electricians, hairdressers, babysitters, drivers, mechanics, and various types of laborers. The self-employed could charge market prices for their goods or services, although price gouging could be punishable; and they would have to pay a tax on their earnings. Hiring labor remained illegal but partnerships were allowed. The only Cubans excluded from self-employment were administrative personnel and new professionals with university degrees (who were both required to work for and guaranteed employment by the state), although expanding self-employment to some professionals outside of health and education was soon under consideration.[29]

Another measure that Cuba's leaders considered regrettable but necessary was the decriminalization, announced in August 1993, of hard currency transactions by the Cuban population.[30] Some hard currency had always circulated in revolutionary Cuba, but, as the "special period" crisis deepened, hard currency poured into the country, especially from tourism and from friends and relatives abroad. Over the course of the special period, the Cuban peso had become almost worthless: the official exchange rate stood at 1.2 pesos per dollar, but the street rate went from seven to fifteen pesos to eighty to 100 pesos per dollar from 1990 to the end of 1993. Cubans still used pesos to buy the bare necessities supplied by the state, but they found it increasingly necessary, just for day-to-day survival, to buy on the flourishing black market with hard currency.

The Cuban leadership decriminalized the holding of hard currency, in large part to enable the state to capture more of it. As the leadership introduced decriminalization, it also rapidly began to expand the country's network of hard currency stores, which had previously been off-limits to Cubans. Now, these increasingly numerous stores would sell to Cubans at prices that were high but lower than those on the black market. The leadership also accompanied decriminalization with plans to supply as many as 500 visas per week to Cuban expatriates, with no restrictions on the amount of hard currency they could bring into the country to spend themselves or to hand over to friends and relatives.[31]

Cuban leaders recognized that these various measures would aggravate inequalities that were based, not on work or other social contributions, but simply on access to hard currency. They argued, however, that although these measures would immediately benefit those with better access—including workers in tourism, prostitutes and pimps, black marketeers, and those lucky enough to have generous, expatriate friends or relatives—everyone would ultimately benefit from the state's ability to capture more hard currency to satisfy social needs.

Cuba's financial problems were also a main topic at the December 1993 National Assembly session.[32] Finance Minister Rodríguez reported that 60 percent of the country's mushrooming budget deficit, which was mentioned above, had been covered by printing new money, and that, while supplies of goods and services had plummeted over the special period, average money incomes had remained stable. As a result, the amount of excess money in circulation was now equal to fourteen months of the population's average wages.

To improve the country's financial balances, Rodríguez proposed (1) systematically reducing state subsidies to enterprises, as mentioned above; (2) increasing interest rates to stimulate savings; (3) imposing personal and business income taxes; and (4) selectively increasing prices. In keeping with the revolutionary leadership's continuing commitment to socialism and social justice, Rodríguez's proposals did not include cutting social security or social services like health and education, or opening the floodgates to capitalism by selling off state enterprises. He also disdained any elements of neoliberal "shock treatment"—overnight currency devaluations, drastic cuts in state spending and services, extortionary price and tax hikes, etc.—with which other Latin American regimes have been ravaging especially their poorer citizens for over a decade.

Still, it was recognized that adjusting Cuba's financial imbalances would entail sacrifices on the part of many; the National Assembly therefore decided to delay making any decisions until these and related issues had been thrashed out in a truly national debate.

The Political Response

This debate began in January 1994. The Cuban labor force (managers and workers) then started to gather in the 80,000 trade union locals for four- to eight-hour meetings to discuss ways to improve efficiency and output in their workplaces and ways to cope nationally with the country's financial imbalances and other economic problems.[33]

Early reports indicate workers expressing anger and frustration about such things as workdays wasted because of lacking raw materials, spare parts, or adequate transportation to and from work; about co-workers who pilfer goods from work and sell them on the black market, and about administrative personnel who either cooperate or look the other way; about medicines, such as insulin, that cannot be found in state pharmacies, but are plentiful in dollar stores; about the fact that, at the current exchange rate on the street, anyone can earn the equivalent of an average month's wage, 198 pesos, by earning just a few dollars; about the fact that prostitutes, speculators, thieves, and those lucky enough to have friends and relatives in the United States have plenty of dollars, but most hard-working Cubans do not; about those who do not come to work regularly or at all in order to play around or to earn a few dollars; and about being fleeced by black marketeers who sometimes sell at 1,000 percent markups. When the National Assembly next acts, it will have before it a grand summary of the complaints, comments, and suggestions that Cuban workers have put forth in these discussions.

Such mass discussions are by no means new in revolutionary Cuba. As was noted in Chapter 4, they have long been a feature of Cuban politics and were written into the Cuban Constitution of 1976. The fact that these meetings are taking place in the midst of the current crisis, however, is worthy of note. It underscores the Cuban leaders' ongoing concern not just with the economics but with the politics of the country's crisis.

Nor is this the first such mass deliberation during the current crisis. The Cuban Communist Party initiated similar discussions leading up to its Fourth Congress, which was held in October 1991. In February and March of 1990, just after Soviet-bloc Communism started to crumble, Cuba's top party leaders announced the coming congress and issued a call (*llamamiento*) to Cubans in and out of the party to enter into nationwide discussions of the country's economic difficulties and of its political structures, which were now slated for rectification.

As these pre-congress discussions were getting underway in April, the revolution's international supporters were falling away and its international enemies were stepping up their harassment—the United States, for example, staged three simultaneous military maneuvers off Cuban shores at the time. The revolution was facing unprecedented challenges, but these discussions, by either bogging down in minutiae or responding to the external threat with revolutionary boosterism, were evading critical issues. As a result, Cuba's leaders soon called these discussions to a halt.

They were restarted in June after the party's political bureau issued the following clarification:

> The limits of discussion can't be fixed beforehand. ... [T]he Call's discussion has a dual purpose: on the one hand, it is a real consultation, where people can express different views; and on the other hand, it's a process of political clarification. We [party members] are not, of course, passive bystanders, simply listening to proposals. What is needed is a dialogue, a confrontation of ideas, where the most convincing, best-argued and defended, win out. Thus, the quality of these meetings can't be measured—as we mistakenly have at

times—by the unanimity reached, or by the absence of points raised that could be considered problematic or divergent.[34]

What ensued was a series of mass discussions that raised a host of criticisms, many of which were directed at Cuba's post-1970 political system (as described in Chapter 4). Concerning the Organs of Popular Power (*Organos de Poder Popular*, or OPP), support was expressed for lawmaking to start more often with grassroots consultations, for increasing municipal OPP delegates' authority to solve problems, for enlivening debate in the National Assembly, and for removing the party from the process of nominating candidates for OPP office.

Concerning mass organizations, like the trade unions, support was expressed for greater bottom-up control and less party interference in the nomination of leaders and in other matters. Concerning the party itself, support was expressed for enlivening internal party debates, for democratizing internal party elections, for returning to co-workers their former say in proposing candidates for party membership, and for allowing religious believers to join the party.[35]

Although Cuba's single-party system never became a serious issue in these mass discussions, outside Cuba it was the main point of controversy. Even before these discussions had gotten underway, government officials, mass media, and Cuban exiles in the United States were making this the focus of their verbal assaults on the revolutionary regime; and the regime, in the personage of Fidel Castro, defended itself publicly. Castro reminded everyone that well before Lenin, Cuba's own José Martí had beseeched his compatriots to unite in a single party to defend their country's independence. Castro warned that if Cubans split up their forces into two or more parties, Washington would intervene with its overpowering wealth and technology, as it had so many times before in this century, to divide and conquer.[36] Due to the highly politicized atmosphere, it is impossible to gauge the level of support that may have then existed in Cuba for a multiparty system; but reportedly, only 1/100 of 1 percent of the participants in the mass discussions leading up to the Fourth Party Congress expressed support for a multiparty system.[37] Still, there was widespread agreement that Cuba's single party, as well as the political system of which it was a part, needed reform.

Even before the Fourth Congress, some important reforms were instituted in party practices. In October 1990, for example, in order to eliminate waste and duplication of efforts, the party's leadership apparatus, from the central committee down to the local branch, was reorganized and drastically cut in size.[38] Internal party elections, which had often consisted of nothing more than a show of hands for an unopposed incumbent or new candidate, were reformed to include rank-and-file nominations and secret balloting. The process of selecting the 1,800 delegates to the Fourth Congress was also reportedly freer of top-level control than similar processes in the past. About one-third of the delegates were elected by local party branches in leading institutions and priority industries; almost two-thirds were nominated by other local branches and elected by secret ballot by provincial party assemblies, and only nine (from Cuban diplomatic missions abroad) were chosen centrally.[39]

The Fourth Congress itself reportedly engaged in considerably more debate than its predecessors. The change was noted by the only foreign journalist present:

> That first day, Fidel Castro laid aside the formal report in favor of an unwritten speech that offered a sobering context for the Congress, but no blueprint. This was the first Congress where not all the votes were unanimous. ... Never has Cuba been under such assault from all sides. For three decades, at the sign of (very real) hostility, the tendency has been to

close ranks in defense of the revolution, no questions asked. Yet, this time the response that won out was to open the door to discussion, divergence of opinion, criticism.[40]

Although some delegates opposed this new openness, others took seriously the revolutionary leadership's call for debate and spoke their minds on the floor of the congress.

By its end, the Fourth Congress had approved a variety of political measures. On the one hand, it gave the party's central committee, headed by President Castro, exceptional powers should a severe and direct internal or external threat emerge. On the other hand, the congress proposed political changes to further open the channels for democratic participation and debate in Cuba.

One set of changes focused on broadening the party's membership base. Most notably, the congress concluded a party discussion of many years[41] by proposing to drop the previous prohibition against religious believers being party members. But equally important, the congress's delegates, 60 percent of whom were under forty-five years of age, lowered the minimum age for party membership; at several points, delegates emphasized that the party now had to unify three generations. The congress also approved returning to the practice of allowing workers to propose co-workers for party membership.

Other changes addressed the various criticisms that had been leveled at the OPP. The congress approved the creation of a new governmental level between municipal OPP assemblies and neighborhood residents, Popular Councils (*Consejos Populares*), designed to aid in addressing local problems more quickly and more effectively. The congress also approved removing the party from the nomination process and replacing indirect with direct elections for provincial and national assemblies.

In July 1992, the National Assembly approved the changes proposed by the Fourth Party Congress and passed new electoral legislation. The following December, municipal elections were held. With neighborhood nominations and at least two candidates standing for every post, these seem to have been conducted in much the same way as previous OPP elections at this level. But the provincial and national elections held in February 1993 differed from past elections. Instead of being nominated by party-led committees, half of the candidates were nominated by municipal delegates from among their number; the other half were nominated by the country's mass organizations, without official party involvement.[42] About one-third of those nominated and, as will become clear presently, of those elected to the provincial and national assemblies were not members of the party or of its youth organization. Party members still predominated in these assemblies, but the new nominating process opened them to greater numbers of non-party members.[43]

The new electoral procedures, however, were in at least one respect more restrictive than their predecessors. As mentioned in Chapter 4, the old electoral law in most instances required the party-led nominating committees to nominate at least 25 percent more candidates than available seats. But in the February elections, the number of candidates nominated just matched the number of seats available.[44] The electorate could reject a candidate by withholding more than half of its votes. But this did not happen in February 1993: all candidates were elected.

The election did have an element of competition, however. Cuba's few, small dissident groups boycotted the elections by refusing to stand for nomination and appealed to all Cubans to reject the regime by casting blank or spoiled ballots. About thirty U.S.-based radio stations broadcast this dissident appeal to the island, and Fidel Castro called on Cubans to vote a "united ballot" to elect the full slate of candidates; both sides approached the February elections as a referendum on the revolutionary regime. According to the official count, of the 98.8 percent of the electorate that voted, only about 7.2 percent (14.3 percent in Havana) cast blank or spoiled ballots and only about 10.4 percent failed to cast a "united ballot."[45] Unofficial, often unfriendly, sources claimed that up to 30 percent of the electorate had not voted a "united ballot." But no one could claim that less than an overwhelming majority of the Cuban people still supported (at the very least, still refused to desert) the revolutionary regime.

Conclusion

Cuba's political system is neither a bourgeois democracy systematically subject to the undemocratic sway of unequally distributed economic resources nor an ideal socialist democracy with unimpeded public rights and empowerment. Political restrictions remain in revolutionary Cuba which, while intended to shield against the machinations of the United States and of other counterrevolutionary enemies, sometimes stifle loyal critics. Overemphasizing such restrictions, however, would obscure the central thrust of recent political reforms in Cuba. Overall, these reforms have further opened the channels for democratic participation and debate within the revolution.

It is important to note that the political response to the "special period" crisis could have been different. Any regime facing severe economic crisis coupled with heightened enemy threats would be tempted to restrict democratic channels and to resort to authoritarian command.[46] But despite the "special period" crisis, this was not the response of the Cuban regime. Even though the Fourth Party Congress approved exceptional powers for the central committee, it sought to broaden and consolidate support and to build greater consensus for dealing with the challenges of the special period by opening political channels further.

This decision is explained, at least in part, by the fact that years of educational progress under the revolution have multiplied the political capabilities and expectations in Cuba. Now more educated, the population not only increasingly possesses the capacity but increasingly demands the opportunity to participate more fully in critical debate and decision-making. This development is not limited to Cuba's new professionals, but it is most clearly symbolized by their rise. In this indirect sense, the new professionals, and the educational expansion they exemplify, have influenced the political response to the "special period" crisis. The new professionals' influence, however, has not been just indirect: Fully 55 percent of the delegates to the Fourth Party Congress, for example, had university degrees; new professionals predominated at the congress, where Cuba's recent political reforms were proposed and debated.[47]

Given the growing economic role of Cuba's new professionals, their expanding political role is not surprising. It only further confirms what has been said already about the new professionals' increasing importance in Cuban society. This importance, moreover, has increased steadily, and will increase even more as new professionals displace the old cadres remaining in intermediate-level posts and as they take over higher-level posts left open as older revolutionary leaders pass on. Regardless of how Cuba's future turns out, the new professionals are increasingly positioned to play a significant part in shaping it.

This is not to say, however, that the new professional stratum is destined to play a unified role in Cuba's future. In the near term, most of the new professionals are likely to continue pressing for greater political openness, to increasingly oppose authoritarian restrictions not required for preventing subversion, and to resist any move toward full-scale authoritarian command not provoked by external aggression.

Beyond this, however, the new professionals are unlikely to speak or act in unison. New professional occupations, after all, range from those of medium-level technicians working on shop floors and in fields to those of high-level administrators working in central state offices. The more advanced diplomas that distinguish the new professionals from others are hardly sufficient to consistently unify the behavior or opinions of the new professionals themselves, spread out as they are over a wide range of occupations. For all their importance as a stratum in Cuban society so far, the new professionals, given their circumstances, are likely to express divergent political views, if and to whatever extent that Cuba's political system should open in the future.

It is possible, in fact, to identify within the new professional stratum three structural positions from which three political groups could potentially arise and begin to attract followers from within the stratum, pulling new professionals into three different political directions.

In the first position are party members, regular members of the security and propaganda apparatus, and party appointees to higher intermediate-level political and economic posts. These new professionals are likely to view their personal and professional fates as closely and directly tied to that of the revolutionary leadership. This is due, among other reasons, to their having positioned themselves, by nature of their work, as potential targets of counterrevolutionary revenge. Although certain of these individuals from time to time defect with great hoopla, the bulk of them are likely to continue supporting the leadership, no matter what.

In the second position sit the top technical, scientific, and managerial personnel; successful artists and writers; and other higher-level new professionals, whose futures are relatively independent of the revolutionary leadership. Although they sometimes head up calls for greater political openness, these new professionals can also exhibit undemocratic tendencies. Sure of their own superior knowledge and worth, these new professionals sometimes favor technocratic and elitist measures that disregard working class interests. If convinced that reverting to capitalism would improve their personal and professional chances, many of these new professionals could come to reject socialism and its achievements altogether.

In the third position are medium-level technicians and others at the lower end of the new professional stratum. Socially close to the working class, these are likely to share Cuban workers' affinity for socialism. Despite the hardships of the special period, they would most likely support the revolutionary leadership so long as it tries to safeguard socialism's achievements. But if the leadership were to desert socialism, these new professionals could find common cause with workers in forming a new socialist opposition.

All of these groups, of course, may never fully form or, if they do, may never reach political significance. The Cuban political process remains affected by important factors—revolutionary consciousness, years of shared experiences, nationalism, and so on—that help to keep the body politic unified. Identifying potential cleavages, however, allows for consideration of major political orientations that could emerge among the new professionals over the next several years.

The more immediate question about Cuba's future, of course, is when will its economy recover. Both foreign and Cuban experts have begun predicting that, barring additional external shocks, the Cuban economy should start to slowly improve by late 1994.[48] But many imponderables remain. As the Secretary to the Council of Ministers, Carlos Lage, has underscored, "how long this recuperation will take, how important it will be, and when it will begin to weigh in the solution of given problems and the population's standard of living" is impossible to know.[49]

Another unknown is whether—and, if so, when—the United States will lift its economic blockade against Cuba. An end to the blockade could help ease both the recovery of the Cuban economy and the immediate suffering of many Cubans. The United States is likely to withdraw its blockade, however, only in response to considerable political pressure. No one, however, should enter this battle under the illusion that ending the blockade will be a panacea for Cuba's economy or its revolution.

The irony of the situation is that lifting the blockade would confront Cuba with difficult challenges. Not only would it lay open the revolution all the more to U.S. political and ideological pressures, but also it would threaten Cuba with again becoming an appendage of the U.S. economy, with what the Cubans are now calling a "third dependency."[50] How the revolutionary regime or its commitment to socialism and its achievements would endure such an onslaught, however, must remain a topic for future writings and an issue for future struggles.

For now, no one can foretell how long Cuba's "special period" crisis will last. But neither can the crisis be regarded conclusively as the revolution's last gasp.

198 The Cuban Revolution in Crisis

Notes

1. For information on the blockade, see Mary Murray, *Cruel and Unusual Punishment: The U.S. Blockade Against Cuba* (Melbourne, Australia: Ocean Press, 1993); and Michael Krinsky and David Galore, eds., *United States Economic Measures Against Cuba: Proceedings in the United Nations and International Law Issues* (Northampton, MA: Aletheia Press, 1993).
2. See *Cuba Business*, June 1991, p. 8.
3. See "Report on Fidel Castro's Speech at the Closing Session of the Fifth National Forum on Spare Parts," *Granma Weekly Review*, 30 December 1990, p. 2.
4. See Marc Frank, *Cuba Looks to the Year 2000* (New York: International Publishers, 1993), p. 143.
5. See Fidel Castro, "Speech to the opening session of Fourth Congress of the Communist Party of Cuba," in Gail Reed, ed., *Island in the Storm: The Cuban Communist Party's Fourth Congress* (Melbourne, Australia: Ocean Press; New York: Center for Cuban Studies, 1992), pp. 25-79.
6. See Andrew Zimbalist, "Dateline Cuba: Hanging on in Havana," *Foreign Policy*, Spring 1993, pp. 151-167.
7. See Susana Lee, "Interview with Carlos Lage," *Granma International*, 10 November 1993, p. 5.
8. For example, see Fidel Castro, "Our Peoples are Learning from Experience What Imperialism, What Capitalism, What Neoliberalism Mean," *Granma Weekly Review*, 16 February 1994, pp. 3-7.
9. See *The Cuba Letter*, April 1994.
10. Lee, p. 6.
11. See *Cuba Business*, Aug. 1991, p. 2; "A Way Out of the Wilderness: An Interview with Fidel Castro," *Euromoney*, July 1992, pp. 40-44; *The Economist* Intelligence Unit, *Cuba: Country Profile* (London: The Economist, Fourth Quarter 1993), p. 15; and "Fidel Castro's Speech at the Fifth UNEAC Congress," *Granma International*, 8 December 1993, pp. 3-4.
12. See *Cuba Business*, October 1991, p. 3; and Nicolás Ríos, "Se resiste para evitar una 'tercera' dependencia: una entrevista con Marcos Portal," *Contrapunto*, 15 November/12 December 1993, pp. 18-28.

13. For excellent overviews of Cuba's biotechnology efforts and much more, see Julie M. Feinsilver, *Healing the Masses: Cuban Health Politics at Home and Abroad* (Berkeley: University of California Press, 1993); and Dalton, *"Everything Within the Revolution".*
14. See Meic Haines, "Scale-Up for Industrial Production," *Cuba Business*, September 1992, p. 2.
15. Some of these difficulties have been well-chronicled in George Grayson, "Cuba: Energy Crisis Tests Revolution," *Petroleum Economist*, September 1992, pp. 11-14; see also "Regional Oil Manoeuvres," *Cuba Business*, February 1992, pp. 6-7.
16. *The Economist* Intelligence Unit, *Cuba: Country Profile*, p. 13.
17. See Lila Haines, "Nuclear Plant Way Behind Schedule," *Cuba Business*, July/August 1992, p. 23
18. Ríos, p. 21.
19. Grayson, p. 13; Lila Haines, "Oil for Survival," *Cuba Business*, June 1992, p. 3; and "Licenses on Offer," *Cuba Business*, January/February 1993, p. 8.
20. For a good overview, see Carmen Diana Deere, "Cuba's Struggle for Self-Sufficiency," *Monthly Review*, July/August 1991, pp. 55-73.
21. See *Granma Weekly Review*, 4 November 1990, p. 3.
22. Frank, pp. 154-55.
23. Angel Ramos, "El Talón de Hambre," *Cambio 16*, 13 May 1993, pp. 81-82.
24. See *Granma International*, 22 September 1993, p.10.
25. Political Bureau of the Communist Party of Cuba, "Resolution: Major Changes in State Agriculture," *Granma International*, 29 September 1993, p. 4; on the precursors to this reform, see *Latin American Weekly Report*, 18 February 1993, p. 75.
26. Lee, p. 7.
27. See *The Cuba Letter*, February 1994.
28. Fidel Castro, "Speech at the Fifth UNEAC Congress," pp. 2-4; see also Castro's remarks as quoted in Rudolfo Casals, "Improving Finances: The Next Objective," *Granma International*, 12 January 1993, pp. 12-13.
29. See Joaquín Oramas, "Regulations for Self-Employment Confirmed and Expanded," *Granma International*, 22 September 1993, p. 12; and Lee, p. 9.

30. For the official announcement, see *Granma International*, 25 August 1993, p. 13.

31. See *Latin American Weekly Report*, 12 August 1993, p. 368; see also Lee, p. 8.

32. Casals, "Improving Finances"; see also *The Cuba Letter*, February 1994.

33. See *The Cuba Letter*, March 1994.

34. Quoted in Reed, p. 16.

35. For these and other criticisms, see Reed, pp. 17-19.

36. See Fidel Castro, "Speech at the Closing of the Special Session of the National Assembly," *Granma Weekly Review*, 4 March 1990; and Fidel Castro, "Speech at the Closing of the Tenth Regular Session of the National Assembly," *Granma International*, 12 January 1992, pp. 2-6.

37. Cited in Reed, p. 18.

38. "Bureaucracy Under Attack," *Cuba Business*, October 1990, p. 1.

39. Reed, p. 20.

40. Ibid., pp. 20-21.

41. For information on this discussion, see Frei Betto, *Fidel y la religion: conversaciones con Frei Betto* (Havana: Consejo de Estado, 1985), pp. 227-50; and Gianni Mina, *Habla Fidel* (Madrid: Mondadori, 1988), pp. 257-59.

42. See *Trabajadores*, 19 October 1992, p. 2.

43. See *Latin American Weekly Report*, 11 March 1993, p. 118; on the extent of party domination of OPP assemblies in the past, see Archibald R.M. Ritter, "The Organs of People's Power and the Communist Party: The Nature of Cuban Democracy," in Halebsky and Kirk, eds., *Cuba: Twenty-Five Years of Revolution* (New York: Praeger, 1985), pp. 270-90.

44. *Latin American Weekly Report*, 11 March 1993, p. 118.

45. Ibid.

46. For an extensive discussion of the issues involved in socialist regimes, see James F. Petras and Frank T. Fitzgerald, "Authoritarianism and Democracy in the Transition to Socialism," *Latin American Perspectives* 15, no. 1 (Winter 1988): 93-111; and Frank T. Fitzgerald and James F. Petras, "Confusion About the Transition to Socialism," *Latin American Perspectives* 15, no. 1 (Winter 1988): 124-33. For an old but still fundamental treatment of bourgeois regimes, see Clinton Rossiter, *Constitutional Dictatorship:*

Crisis Government in the Modern Democracies (Princeton NJ: Princeton University Press, 1948).

47. See *Granma International*, 20 October 1991.

48. See, for example, *The Economist* Intelligence Unit, *Cuba: Country Report*, p. 10; and Lee, p. 9.

49. Ibid.

50. Ríos, *passim.*

Selected Bibliography

Cuban Periodicals

Bohemia
Cuba Socialista
Cuestiones de la Economía Plantficada
Economía y Desarrollo
Educación
El Economista
Granma
Granma International
Granma Weekly Review
Revista Cubana de Derecho
Sobre Educación Superior
Trabajadores
Universidad de la Habana

OFFICIAL CUBAN DOCUMENTS

Asociación Nacional de Economistas de Cuba. "Constitución." *Economía y Desarrollo* 52 (March/April 1979): 24-83.

Comité Estatal Estadística. *Compendio anuario estadístico de la República de Cuba, 1976.* Havana: 1976.

_____. *Compendio anuario estadístico de la República de Cuba, 1984.* Havana: 1984.

Comité Estatal Estadística, Dirección de Demografía. *Encuesta demografía nacional de 1979—metodología y tablas seleccionades.* Havana: 1981.

_____. *Encuesta demografía nacional de 1979: principales características laborales de la población de Cuba.* Havana: 1981.

_____. *Anuario Estadístico de Cuba.* Havana: 1984.

Consejo Superior de Universidades. *La reforma de la enseñanza superior en Cuba.* Havana: 1962.

Constitution of the Republic of Cuba. New York: Center for Cuban Studies, 1976.

Federación de Mujeres Cubanas. *Cuban Women in Higher Education.* Havana: Editorial Letras Cubanas, 1985.

Junta Central de Planificación. *Segunda plenaria nacional de chequeo de la implantación del SDPE.* Havana: Ediciones JUCEPLAN, 1980.

"Ley que crea el Ministerio de Educación Superior." *Universidad de la Habana,* nos. 203/204 (1976): 171-175.

Memoirs: Second Congress of the Association of Third World Economists. Havana: Editorial de Ciencias Sociales, 1982.

Memorias del XIII Congreso de la CTC. Havana: 1973.

Ministerio de Educación. *Cuba: organización de la educación, 1981-1983, informe a la XXXIX Conferencia Internacional de Educación, Genebra, Suiza.* Havana: 1984.

_____. *Documentos directivas para el perfeccionamiento del Sistema Nacional de Educación.* Havana: 1975.

_____. *Informe a la Asamblea Nacional del Poder Popular.* Havana: 1981.

_____. *Informe de la delegación de la República de Cuba a la VII Conferencia de Minstros de Educación Superior y Media Especializadas de los Países Socialistas.* Havana 1972.

_____. *El plan de perfeccionamiento y desarrollo del Sistema Nacional de Educación de Cuba.* Havana: 1976.

_____. *El principio de la combinación del trabajo en la educación superior: Informe a la Conferencia de Ministros de Educación Superior de Países Socialistas.* Havana: 1974.

Oficina Nacional de los Censos Demográfica y Electora. *Censos de población, viviendos y electoral.* Havana: 1953.

Political Bureau of the Communist Party of Cuba, "Resolution: Major Changes in State Agriculture," *Granma International,* 29 September 1993, pp. 4.

Primer Congreso del Partido Comunista de Cuba. *Tesis y resoluciones.* Havana: Editorial de Ciencias Sociales, 1978.

Reglamento de las Asambleas Nacional, Provincial, y Municipal del Poder Popular. Havana: Editorial Obre, 1979.

Second Congress of the Communist Party of Cuba. *Documents and Speeches.* Havana: Political Publishers, 1981.

Segunda plenaria nacional de chequeo de la implantación del SDPE. Havana: Ediciones JUCEPLAN, 1980.

Books, Articles, and Other Materials

Azicri, Max. *Cuba: Politics, Economics and Society.* London: Pinter Publishers, 1988.

Bach, Robert L. "The New Cuban Immigrants: Their Background and Prospects." In U.S. House of Representatives, Committee on the Judiciary, *Caribbean Migration,* 96th Congress, 1980.

Bach, Robert, et al. "The Flotilla 'Entrants': Latest and Most Controversial." *Cuban Studies/Estudios Cubanos* 11/12 (July 1981/January 1982): 29-48.

Bengelsdorf, Carollee. "A Large School of Government." *Cuba Review* 6, no. 3 (September 1976): 6-18.

_____. "Between Vision and Reality: Democracy in Socialist Theory and Practice." Ph.D. diss., Massachusetts Institute of Technology, 1985.

_____. "On the Problem of Studying Women in Cuba," in *Cuban Political Economy: Controversies in Cubanology,* edited by Andrew Zimbalist, pp. 119-136. Boulder, CO: Westview Press, 1989.

Benjamin, Medea, et al. *No Free Lunch: Food and Revolution in Cuba Today.* San Francisco: Institute for Food and Development Policy, 1984.

Betto, Frei. *Fidel on Religion.* Sydney, Australia: Pathfinder Press, 1986.

Blumenthal, Hans, and Haydée García, eds., *Formación profesional en Latinoamérica.* Caracas: Editorial Nueva Sociedad, 1987.

Bonachea, Rolando, and Nelson Valdés, eds. *Cuba in Revolution.* Garden City, NY: Doubleday, 1972.

Boorstein, Edward. *The Economic Transformation of Cuba.* New York: Monthly Review Press, 1968.

Bray, Donald W., and Timothy F. Harding. "Cuba." In *Latin Amer-*

ica: The Struggle with Dependency and Beyond, edited by Ronald H. Chilcote and Joel C. Edelstein, pp. 579-734. Cambridge, MA: Schenkman Publishing, 1974.

Brundenius, Claes. *Economic Growth, Basic Needs and Income Distribution in Revolutionary Cuba.* Lund, Sweden: University of Lund, 1981.

_____. *Revolutionary Cuba: The Challenge of Growth with Equity.* Boulder, CO: Westview Press, 1984.

_____. "Some Notes on the Development of the Cuban Labor Force 1979-80." *Cuban Studies/Estudios Cubanos* 13, no. 2 (Summer 1983): 65-77.

Brundenius, Claes, and Andrew Zimbalist. *The Cuban Economy: Measurement and Analysis of Socialist Performance.* Baltimore: The Johns Hopkins Press, 1989.

Brunner, Heinrich. *Cuban Sugar Policy from 1963 to 1970.* Pittsburgh: University of Pittsburgh Press, 1977.

Bukharin, Nikolai. *The Economics of the Transformation Period.* New York: Bergman, 1971.

Casal, Lourdes. "Cuban Communist Party: The Best Among the Good." *Cuba Review* 6, no. 3 (September 1976): 24-27.

_____. "On Popular Power: The Organization of the Cuban State during the Period of Transition." *Latin American Perspectives*, Supplement 1975: 78-99.

Castro, Fidel. *Fidel Castro Speaks*, edited by Martin Kenner and James Petras. New York: Grove Press, 1969.

_____. *Fidel Castro Speeches. Vol. 2: Our Power Is That of the Working People*, edited by Michael Taber. New York: Pathfinder Press, 1983.

_____. *Fidel in Chile.* New York: International Publishers, 1975.

_____. *Main Report to the First Congress of the Communist Party of Cuba.* Havana: Communist Party of Cuba, 1977.

_____. "Main Report to the Third Congress of the Communist Party of Cuba," *Granma Weekly Review*, 16 February 1986.

_____. "Report on the Cuban Economy." In *Cuba in Revolution*, edited by Rolando Bonachea and Nelson Valdés, pp. 317-56. Garden City, NY: Doubleday, 1972.

_____. "Revolutionary Consciousness and the Fight Against Corruption." In *Fidel Castro Speeches, Vol. 2: Our Power Is That of the Working People,* edited by Michael Taber. (New York: Pathfinder Press, 1983).

_____. "Speech at the Close of the Deferred Session of the Third Congress of the Communist Party of Cuba." *Granma Weekly Review,* 14 December 1986.

_____. "Speech to the Opening Session of Fourth Congress of the Communist Party of Cuba." In *Island in the Storm: The Cuban Communist Party's Fourth Congress* by Gail Reed, pp. 25–79. Melbourne, Australia: Ocean Press; New York: Center for Cuban Studies, 1992.

_____. "We Will Never Build a Communist Conscience with a Dollar Sign in the Minds and Hearts of Men." In *Fidel Castro Speaks,* edited by Martin Kenner and James Petras, pp. 199–221. New York: Grove Press, 1969.

_____. *World Economic and Social Crisis.* Havana: The Council of State, 1983.

Castro, Raúl. "Three Speeches Against Bureaucracy." In *Fidel Castro Speeches, Vol. 2,* edited by Michael Taber, pp. 280–98. New York: Pathfinder Press, 1983.

CEPAL. *Cuba: estilo de desarrollo y políticos sociales.* Cerro del Agua, México: Siglo Veintiuno Editores, 1980.

Clark, Juan M. "The Exodus from Revolutionary Cuba (1959–1974): A Sociological Analysis." Ph.D diss., University of Florida, 1975.

Cockburn, Cynthia. "People's Power." In *Cuba: The Second Decade,* edited by John Griffiths and Peter Griffiths, pp. 18–35. London: Writers and Readers Publishing Cooperative, 1979.

Dalton, Thomas C. *"Everything Within the Revolution": Cuban Strategies for Social Development Since 1960.* Boulder, CO: Westview Press, 1993.

Deere, Carmen Diana. "Cuba's Struggle for Self-Sufficiency." *Monthly Review,* July/August 1991, pp. 55-73.

Demographic Yearbook, Historical Supplement. New York: United Nations Organization, 1979.

Díaz-Briquets, Sergio, and Lisandro Pérez. *Cuba: The Demography of Revolution.* Washington, DC: The Population Reference Bureau, 1981.

Domínguez, Jorge. *Cuba: Order and Revolution.* Cambridge: Harvard University Press, 1978.

Dorticós, Osvaldo. *Discurso en el acto de presentación de los militantes del Partido del Instituto de Economía.* Havana: Editorial de Ciencias Sociales, 1969.

Dumoulin, John, and Isabel Larguia. "Women's Equality and the Cuban Revolution." In *Women and Change in Latin America,* edited by June Nash and Helen Safa, pp. 344-68. South Hadley, MA: Bergin & Garvey Publishers, 1986.

Dumont, René. *Is Cuba Socialist?* New York: Viking Press, 1974.

The Economist Intelligence Unit. *Cuba: Country Profile, 1992-93.* London: *The Economist,* Fourth Quarter 1993.

Espin, Vilma. *Cuban Women Confront the Future.* Melbourne, Australia: Ocean Press; and New York: Center for Cuban Studies, 1992.

Fagen, Richard. *The Transformation of Political Culture in Cuba.* Stanford, CA: Stanford University Press, 1969.

Fagen, Richard, et al. *Cubans in Exile: Disaffection and Revolution.* Stanford, CA: Stanford University Press, 1968.

Feinsilver, Julie M. *Healing the Masses: Cuban Health Politics at Home and Abroad.* Berkeley: University of California Press, 1993.

Ferreira Báez, Francisco. "El sistema de formación profesional de nivel medio en Cuba." In *Formación profesional en Latinoamérica,* edited by Haydée García and Hans Blumenthal, pp. 111-38. Caracas: Editorial Nueva Sociedad, 1987.

Figueroa, Max, et al. *The Basic Secondary School in the Countryside: An Educational Innovation in Cuba.* Paris: UNESCO, 1974.

Fitzgerald, Frank T. "A Critique of the 'Sovietization of Cuba' Thesis." *Science & Society* 42 (Spring 1978): 1-32.

_____. "Cuba's New Professionals." In *Transformation and Struggle: Cuba Faces the 1990s,* edited by Sandor Halebsky and John M. Kirk, pp. 189-203. New York: Praeger, 1990.

_____. *Managing Socialism: From Old Cadres to New Professionals in Revolutionary Cuba.* New York: Praeger, 1990.

_____. "Politics and Social Structure in Revolutionary Cuba: From the Demise of the Old Middle Class to the Rise of the New Professionals." Ph.D. diss., State University of New York at Binghamton, 1985.

_____. "The Reform of the Cuban Economy, 1976-1986: Organisation, Incentives and Patterns of Behaviour." Journal of Latin American Studies 21, no. 2 (May 1989): 283-310.

_____. "The 'Sovietization of Cuba Thesis' Revisited." In *Cuban Political Economy: Controversies in Cubanology*, edited by Andrew Zimbalist, pp. 137-53. Boulder, CO: Westview Press, 1988; and in *Science & Society* 51, no. 4 (Winter 1987/1988): 439-57.

Fitzgerald, Frank T., and James F. Petras. "Confusion About the Transition to Socialism." *Latin American Perspectives* 15, no. 1 (Winter 1988): 124-33.

Frank, Marc. *Cuba Looks to the Year 2000.* New York: International Publishers, 1993.

Friedson, Eliot. "The Theory of Professions: State of the Art." In *The Sociology of the Professions*, edited by Robert Dingwall and Philip Lewis, pp. 19-37. London: Macmillan, 1983.

Fuller, Linda. "Changes in the Relationship Among Unions, Administration, and the Party at the Cuban Workplace, 1959-1982." *Latin American Perspectives* 13, no. 2 (Spring 1986): 6-32.

_____. "Fieldwork in Forbidden Terrain: The U.S. State and the Case of Cuba," *The American Sociologist* 19, no. 2 (Summer 1988): 99-120.

_____. "The Politics of Workers' Control in Cuba, 1959-1983: The Work Center and the National Arena." Ph.D. diss., University of California at Berkeley, 1985.

_____. *Work and Democracy in Socialist Cuba.* Philadelphia: Temple University Press, 1992.

García, Concepción, and Eugene F. Provenzano. "Exiled Teachers and the Cuban Revolution." *Cuban Studies/Estudios Cubanos* 13, no. 1 (Winter 1983): 1-15.

García, Haydée, and Hans Blumenthal, eds. *Formación profesional en Latinoamérica.* Caracas: Editorial Nueva Sociedad, 1987.

Grayson, George. "Cuba: Energy Crisis Tests Revolution." *Petroleum Economist*, September 1992, pp. 11-14.

Griffiths, Franklin, and H. Gordon Skilling. *Interest Groups in Soviet Politics.* Princeton, NJ: Princeton University Press, 1971.

Guevara, Ernesto Che. "Against Bureaucratism." In *Venceremos! The Speeches and Writings of Che Guevara*, edited by John Gerassi, pp. 220-25. New York: Simon and Schuster, 1968.

_____. "Man and Socialism in Cuba." In *Man and Socialism in*

Cuba: The Great Debate edited by Bertram Silverman, pp. 337-54. New York: Atheneum, 1973.

_____. "On the Budgetary Finance System." In *Man and Socialism in Cuba: The Great Debate*, edited by Bertram Silverman, pp. 122-56. New York: Atheneum, 1973.

Haines, Meic. "Scale-Up for Industrial Production." *Cuba Business*, September 1992, p. 2.

Haines, Lila. "Nuclear Plant Way Behind Schedule." *Cuba Business*, July/August 1992, p. 2.

Haines, Lila. "Oil for Survival." *Cuba Business*, June 1992, p. 3.

Halebsky, Sandor, and John M. Kirk, eds. *Cuba: Twenty-Five Years of Revolution.* New York: Praeger, 1985.

_____. *Transformation and Struggle: Cuba Faces the 1990s.* New York: Praeger, 1990.

Harnecker, Marta. *Cuba: Dictatorship or Democracy?* Westport, CT: Lawrence Hill, 1980.

Herrara, Antonio José, and Hernan Rosenkranz. "Political Consciousness in Cuba." In *Cuba: The Second Decade*, edited by John Griffiths and Peter Griffiths, pp. 36-52. London: Writers and Readers Cooperative, 1979.

Huberman, Leo, and Paul Sweezy. *Socialism in Cuba.* New York: Monthly Review Press, 1969.

Huteau, Michel, and Jacques Lautrey. *L'Éducation à Cuba.* Paris: François Maspero, 1973.

Karol, K.S. *Guerrillas in Power: The Course of the Cuban Revolution.* New York: Hill and Wang, 1970.

Kirk, John M., and Sandor Halebsky, eds. *Cuba: Twenty-Five Years Revolution.* New York: Praeger, 1985.

_____. *Transformation and Struggle: Cuba Faces the 1990s.* New York: Praeger, 1990.

Kolesnikov, Nikolai. *Cuba: educación popular y preparación de los cuadros nacionales, 1959-1982.* Moscow; Editorial Progreso, 1983.

Kornai, Janos. *Contradictions and Dilemmas.* Cambridge: Massachusetts Institute of Technology Press, 1986.

_____. *Economics of Shortage.* Amsterdam: North-Holland, 1980.

Krinsky, Michael and David Galore, eds. *United States Economic Measures Against Cuba: Proceedings in the United Nations and International Law Issues.* Northampton, MA: Aletheia Press, 1993.

Lee, Susana. "Interview with Carlos Lage," *Granma International,* 10 November 1993, pp. 4-9.

Leiner, Marvin. *Children Are the Revolution.* New York: Penguin Books, 1978.

_____. "Cuba's Schools: Twnety-five Years Later." In *Cuba: Twenty-Five Years of Revolution,* edited by Sandor Halebsky and John M. Kirk, pp. 27-44. New York: Praeger, 1985.

León, Laureano. "Hacia la eficacia económica." *América Latina,* January 1989, pp. 4-9.

Lockwood, Lee. *Castro's Cuba, Cuba's Fidel.* New York: Vintage Books, 1969.

Luxemburg, Rosa. "What is Economics?" In *Rosa Luxemburg Speaks,* edited by Mary-Alice Waters, pp. 219-45. New York: Pathfinder Press, 1970.

MacEwan, Arthur. "Incentives, Equality, and Power in Revolutionary Cuba." In *The New Cuba,* edited by Ronald Radosh, pp. 74-101. New York: Morrow, 1976.

_____. *Revolution and Economic Development in Cuba.* New York: St. Martin's Press, 1981.

Martel, Raúl. *La empresa socialista.* Havana: Editorial de Ciencias Sociales, 1979.

Martínez Heredia, Fermando. *Rectificación y profundización del socialismo en Cuba.* Buenos Aires: Ediciones Dialéctica. 1989.

Mesa-Lago, Carmelo. *Cuba in the 1970s: Pragmatism and Institutionalization.* Albuquerque: University of New Mexico Press, 1974.

_____. "Economic Significance of Unpaid Labor in Socialist Cuba." *Industrial and Labor Relations Review* 22 (April 1969): 339-57.

_____. *The Economy of Socialist Cuba.* Albuquerque: University of New Mexico Press, 1981.

_____. *The Labor Force, Employment, Unemployment and Underemployment in Cuba: 1899-1970.* Beverly Hills, CA: Sage Publications, 1972.

Mina, Gianni. *Habla Fidel.* Madrid: Mondadori, 1988.

Morley, Morris H. *Imperial State and Revolution: The United*

States and Cuba, 1952-1986. Cambridge, MA: Cambridge University Press, 1987.

_____. "Toward a Theory of Imperial Politics: United States Policy and the Processes of State Formation, Disintegration and Consolidation in Cuba, 1898-1978." Ph.D. diss., State University of New York at Binghamton, 1980.

Morley, Morris, and James Petras. "Cuban Socialism: Rectification and the New Model of Accumulation." In their *Latin America in the Time of Cholera*, pp. 93-127. New York: Routledge, Chapman and Hall, 1992.

Murray, Mary. *Cruel and Unusual Punishment: The U.S. Blockade Against Cuba.* Melbourne, Australia: Ocean Press, 1993.

Nash, June, and Helen Safa, eds. *Women and Change in Latin America.* South Hadley, MA: Bergin & Garvey Publishers, 1986.

Pérez, Humberto. *Sobre las dificultades objectivas de la revolución: lo que el pueblo deber saber.* Havana: Editorial Política, 1979.

Pérez-Stable, Marifeli. "Institutionalization and the Workers' Response." *Cuban Studies/Estudios Cubanos* 6, no. 2 (July 1976): 31-54.

_____. "Politics and *Conciencia* in Revolutionary Cuba, 1959-1984." Ph.D. diss., State University of New York at Stony Brook, 1985.

_____. "Whither the Cuban Working Class?" *Latin American Perspectives*, Supplement 1975: 60-77.

Petras, James F. and Frank T. Fitzgerald. "Authoritarianism and Democracy in the Transition to Socialism." *Latin American Perspectives* 15, no. 1 (Winter 1988): 93-111.

Petras, James and Morris Morley. "Cuban Socialism: Rectification and the New Model of Accumulation." In their *Latin America in the Time of Cholera*, pp. 93-127. New York: Routledge, Chapman and Hall, 1992.

Portes, Alejandro, et al. "The New Wave: A Statistical Profile of Recent Cuban Exiles to the United States." *Cuban Studies/Estudios Cubanos* 7, no. 1 (January 1977): 1-32.

Rabkin, Rhoda. *Cuban Politics: The Revolutionary Experiment.* New York: Praeger, 1991.

Randall, Margaret. *Gathering Rage: The Failure of 20th Century*

Revolutions to Develop a Feminist Agenda. New York: Monthly Review Press, 1992.

Reed, Gail. *Island in the Storm: The Cuban Communist Party's Fourth Congress.* Melbourne, Australia: Ocean Press; New York: Center for Cuban Studies, 1992.

Ríos, Nicolás. "Se resiste para evitar una 'tercera' dependencia: una entrevista con Marcos Portal," *Contrapunto,* 15 November/12 December 1993, pp. 18-28.

Ritter, Archibald R.M. *The Economic Development of Revolutionary Cuba.* New York: Praeger, 1974.

_____. "The Organs of People's Power and the Communist Party: The Nature of Cuban Democracy." In *Cuba: Twenty-Five Years of Revolution, 1959-1985,* edited by Sandor Halebsky and John M. Kirk, eds., pp. 270-90. New York: Praeger, 1985.

Roca, Sergio. "State Enterprises in Cuba Under the New System of Planning and Management (SDPE)." *Cuban Studies/Estudios Cubanos* 16 (1986): 153-79.

Rodríguez, Carlos Rafael. *Palabras en los setenta.* Havana: Editorial de Ciéncias Sociales, 1984.

Rosenberg, Jonathan. "Cuba's Free Market Experiment," *Latin American Research Review* 27, no. 3 (1992): 51-89.

Seers, Dudley, ed. *Cuba: The Economic and Social Revolution.* Chapel Hill: University of North Carolina Press, 1964.

Silverman, Bertram, ed. *Man and Socialism in Cuba: The Great Debate.* New York: Atheneum, 1973.

Skilling, H. Gordon. "The Party, Opposition, and Interest Groups in Communist Politics." In *The Soviet Union: A Half-Century of Communism,* edited by Kurt London, pp. 119-49. Baltimore: The Johns Hopkins Press, 1968.

_____, and Franklin Griffiths. *Interest Groups in Soviet Politics.* Princeton, NJ: Princeton University Press, 1971.

Stubbs, Jean. *Cuba: The Test of Time.* London: Latin America Bureau: 1989.

Suchlicki, Jaime. *University Students and Revolution in Cuba, 1910-1968.* Coral Gables, FL: University of Miami Press, 1968.

Tablada, Carlos. *Che Guevara: Economics and Politics in the Transition to Socialism.* Sydney, Australia: Pathfinder/Pacific and Asia, 1989.

Thomas, Hugh. *Cuba: The Pursuit of Freedom.* New York: Harper and Row, 1971.

UNCTAD. *Health and Education Technology in Cuba.* New York: United Nations Organization, 1979.

Valdés, Nelson P. *Cuba: socialismo democrático o bureaucratismo collectivista.* Bogotá: Ediciones Tercer Mundo, 1973.

_____. "The Cuban Revolution: Economic Organization and Bureaucracy." *Latin American Perspectives* 20 (Winter 1979): 13–37.

Wald, Karen. *Children of Che.* Palo Alto, CA: Ramparts Press, 1978.

Weber, Max. "Bureaucracy." In *From Max Weber: Essays in Sociology,* edited by Hans Gerth and C. Wright Mills, eds., pp. 196–244. New York: Oxford University Press, 1959.

Zeitlin, Maurice. *Revolutionary Politics and the Cuban Working Class.* New York: Harper and Row, 1970.

Zimbalist, Andrew. "Cuban Economic Planning: Organization and Performance." In *Cuba: Twenty-Five Years of Revolution,* edited by Sandor Halebsky and John M. Kirk, pp. 213–30. New York: Praeger, 1985.

_____. "Dateline Cuba: Hanging on in Havana," *Foreign Policy* 90 (Spring 1993): 151–167.

_____. "Teetering on the Brink: Cuba's Current Economic and Political Crisis," *Journal of Latin American Studies* 24: 407–418.

_____. "Workers' Participation in Cuba." *Challenge,* November/December 1975, pp. 45–54.

_____, ed. *Cuban Political Economy: Controversies in Cubanology.* Boulder, CO: Westview Press, 1989.

Appendix
Tables for
Chapters 2 through 5

Table 2.1
Estimated Occupational Distribution of Cuban Refugee and Non-refugee Labor Force Participants, 1959-1962

	A	B	C	D	E		F		G
			REFUGEES 1959-1962					REMAINING IN CUBA 1962	
	1953	1959	Registered in U.S.	Unregistered in U.S.	In Other Countries	Total	% of 1959 Total	Total	% of 1959 Total
Intermediate- (and Higher-) Level Occupations									
Lawyers and Judges	7,858	9,126	1,695	925	226	2,846	31.2%	6,280	68.8%
Professional and Semiprofessional	78,051	90,646	12,124	6,615	1,617	20,356	22.5	70,290	77.5
Managers and Executives	93,662	108,776	6,771	3,694	903	11,368	10.4	97,408	89.6
Subtotal	179,571	208,548	20,590	11,234	2,746	34,570	16.6	173,978	83.4
Lower-Level Occupations									
Clerical and Sales	264,569	307,262	17,123	6,901	2,074	26,098	8.5	281,164	91.5
Domestics, Military, and Police	160,406	186,291	4,801	1,935	581	7,317	3.9	178,974	96.1
Unskilled, Semi-Skilled, and Skilled	526,168	611,076	11,301	4,554	1,369	17,224	2.8	593,852	97.2
Agriculture and Fishing	807,514	937,823	1,539	620	186	2,345	0.3	935,478	99.7
Subtotal	1,758,657	2,042,452	34,764	14,010	4,210	52,984	2.6	1,989,468	97.4
Total Labor Force	1,938,228	2,251,000	55,354	25,244	6,956	87,554	3.9	2,163,446	96.1
Total Population/Refugees	5,829,029	6,901,000	169,693	77,387	20,920	268,000	3.9	6,633,000	96.1

Sources: Column A: Labor force from 1953 Cuban Census as categorized by Richard Fagen, et. al., *Cubans in Exile: Disaffection and Revolution* (Stanford: Stanford University Press, 1968), Table 2.1, p. 19; population total from *Compendio anuario estadistico de la Republica de Cuba, 1976* (Cuba: Comite Estatal de Estadisticos, 1976), Table 6, p. 9.

Column B: Population total from *Demographic Yearbook*, Historical Supplement (New York: United Nations Organization, 1979); labor force total is the year's average as reported by Carmelo Mesa-Lago, *The Labor Force, Employment, Unemployment and Underemployment in Cuba: 1899-1970* (Beverly Hills: Sage Publications, 1972), Table 12, p.36; occupational figures estimated by the author based on assumption that each occupational category grew at the same rate as labor force as a whole from 1953 to 1959.

Column C: Labor force from Fagen, *Cubans in Exile*, Table 2.1, p. 19, study of refugee households, registered with the Cuban Refugee Center in Miami; total registered refugees estimated by author based on assumption that proportion of labor force participants in total registered refugee population same as proportion of labor force participants in total Cuban population in 1959, i.e., 32.62 percent.

Column D: Total unregistered refugee figure equals total registered refugee figure subtracted from 247,080, the estimate of total Cuban refugees arriving in the United States between 1959 and 1962 in Juan M. Clark, *The Exodus from Revolutionary Cuba (1959-1974): A Sociological Analysis* (University of Florida, Ph.D. diss., 1975), Table 3, p. 74; total refugee figure explained under column C, above; estimated occupational distribution figures based on widely held assumption that unregistered refugees were on the average better off than their registered counterparts and therefore more likely to come from the intermediate-level occupations. To derive these figures, I put 44.5 percent of the estimated labor force total into the intermediate-level category and 55.5 percent into the lower-level category, in accordance with Clark's estimate, pp. 214-215; I then assumed that these categories were distributed among their subtotals in the same proportions as in columns A through C.

Column E: Total refugees to non-U.S. countries from figures in columns C and D subtracted from 268,000, the estimate of total Cuban refugees to all countries between 1959 and 1962 in Clark, *The Exodus*, Table 3, p. 74; total labor force derived in the same fashion as the counterpart figure in column C, as explained above; occupational distribution figures based on assumption that refugees to countries other than the U.S. had occupational characteristics similar to refugees to the U.S. To derive these figures, I divided the estimated refugee labor force into 39.48 percent intermediate-level and 60.52 percent lower-level positions, the weighted average percentages for columns C and D together.

Column F: Estimated numbers the sums of columns C, D and E; estimated percentages derived by dividing column F by Column B.

Column G: Estimated numbers the remainders of column B minus column F; estimated percentages derived by dividing column G by column B. To facilitate comparison with the base line year 1959, this column does not take into account labor force growth from 1959 to 1962.

Note: As parenthetically indicated on the table, some proportion of individuals in the Managers and Executives, Lawyers and Judges, and Professionals and Semi-Professionals occupational categories would appropriately be considered, not intermediate-level, but higher-level personnel. These latter would include large property owners and their close associates, the Cuban "bourgeoisie." Unfortunately, the census offers no way to separate these out. Although practically the whole Cuban bourgeoisie left in the early exodus, it was relatively small. Therefore, for the purpose at hand, it can be ignored, and these occupational categories can be considered intermediate-level, without introducing any great distortion.

Table 2.2
Estimated Cuban Refugee Labor Force Participants from Intermediate-Level Occupations, 1959-1980

	1959-1962	1963-1965	1966-1968	1969-1971	1972-1974	1975-1977	1978-1980	TOTAL
Refugees	268,000	81,000	174,000	153,000	41,000	19,482	146,376	882,858
Refugee Labor Force Participants	87,554	26,422	56,785	49,909	13,374	6,355	47,748	288,147
Refugees from Intermediate- (and Higher-) Level Occupations	34,570	8,925	10,858	7,332	1,872	810	5,491	69,858
Cumulative Total of Refugees from Intermediate- (and Higher-) Level Occupations	34,570	43,495	54,353	61,685	63,557	64,367	69,858	69,858
Refugees from Intermediate-Level Occupations as a Proportion of 1959 Cuban Intermediate-Level Occupations	16.6%	20.9%	26.1%	29.6%	30.5%	30.9%	33.5%	33.5%

Sources: Refugee total for 1959-1962 from Table 2.1; for 1963-1974, from Clark, *The Exodus*, Table 3, p. 74; for 1975-1980, from Sergio Díaz-Briquets and Lisandro Pérez, *Cuba: The Demography of Revolution* (Washington, D.C.: The Population Reference Bureau, 1981), Table 8, p. 26, increased by 11 percent to account for refugees to countries other than the United States, using Clark's average increment for 1959–1974. Refugee Labor Force Participant figure for 1959–1962 from Table 2.1; for 1963–1980, 32.62 percent of the corresponding refugee figure, in accordance with rationale given under Table 2.1, column C. Refugees from Intermediate- (and Higher-) Level Occupations for 1959–1962 from Table 2.1; for 1963–1974, computed from the percentages of "professionals" among the refugee labor force participants given by Clark, *The Exodus*, Figure 6., p. 74; for 1975–1977, estimated by the author at 12.75 percent, the average of Clark's figure for 1974 and the figure for 1980 in Robert L. Bach, et al., "The Flotilla 'Entrants': Latest and Most Controversial," *Cuban Studies/Estudios Cubanos*, 11/12 (July 1981–January 1982), Table 6, p. 43; for 1978–1980, estimated at 11.5 percent following the findings of Bach. Refugees from Intermediate-Level Occupations as a Proportion of 1959 Intermediate-Level Occupations figures are the Cumulative Total of Refugee Intermediate-Level Occupation figures divided by the total 1959 Intermediate-Level Occupations in Table 2.1, namely 208,548.

Table 3.1
Adult, Primary, Secondary, and Higher Education Enrollments in Cuba, 1958/1959 to 1969/1970

Year	Adult	Primary	Secondary	Higher[a]
1958/1959	N.A.	625,729	88,135	N.A.
1959/1960	N.A.	950,217	90,660	25,295
1960/1961	66,577	1,029,923	122,897	19,454
1961/1962	439,042	1,088,016	151,826	17,888
1962/1963	499,925	1,137,479	182,981	17,257
1963/1964	476,328	1,225,539	216,849	20,393
1964/1965	842,024	1,246,381	217,014	26,271
1965/1966	574,683	1,242,256	231,317	26,162
1966/1967	451,499	1,266,240	255,127	28,243
1967/1968	499,980	1,279,695	288,748	29,238
1968/1969	373,211	1,341,728	276,303	32,327
1969/1970	306,917	1,427,607	276,209	34,520

Source: Ministerio de Educación, *Informe a la Asamblea Nacional del Poder Popular* (Havana: 1981), pp. 344–47

a. Includes all university-level day, evening, and correspondence courses.

Table 3.2
Primary, Secondary, and Higher Education Enrollments as a Percentage of Total Enrollments in Cuba, 1959/1960 and 1970/1971

School Year	Primary	Secondary	Higher	Total
1959–1960	89.1%	8.5%	2.4%	100%
1970–1971	83.3	14.8	1.9	100

Source: Author's computations base on Ministerio de Educación, *Informe a la Asamblea Nacional del Poder Popular* (Havana: 1981), pp. 344–46.

Table 3.3

Cuban Higher Education Enrollments by Subject Area, 1959/1960 and 1969/1970

Subject Area	1959/1960	1969/1970	% Change
Agricultural Sciences	759	5,154	579.1%
Technology	3,211	7,948	147.5
Natural and Exact Sciences	1,479	3,420	131.2
Medical Sciences	3,947	7,977	102.1
Humanities, Social Sciences, and Art	3,757	2,178	-42.0
Education	5,180	1,627	-68.6
Economic Studies	5,144	1,214	-76.4
Total	23,478	29,518	25.7

Source: Ministerio de Educación Superior, *Informe de la delegación de la Republica de Cuba a la VII Conferencia de Ministros de Educación Superior y Media Especializada de los Países Socialistas* (Havana: 1972), pp. 117-18. All percentage change figures computed by author.

Note: The total enrollment figures from this source are somewhat lower than those in Table 3.1. The most likely reason for this discrepancy is that this source may not include some categories of higher education enrollments, such as in correspondence courses. This source is used here because it gives a breakdown of enrollment by "Faculty," labeled "Subject Area" on this table.

Table 4.1

Adult, Primary, Secondary, and Higher Education Enrollments
in Cuba, 1970/1971 to 1984/1985

School Year	Adult	Primary	Secondary	Higher[a]
1970/1971	316,896	1,530,376	272,193	35,137
1971/1972	326,048	1,631,187	282,279	36,877
1972/1973	398,048	1,733,208	324,401	48,735
1973/1974	445,798	1,780,775	395,544	55,435
1974/1975	413,847	1,801,191	520,295	68,051
1975/1976	597,596	1,795,752	629,197	83,957
1976/1977	701,259	1,747,738	806,049	110,148
1977/1978	605,247	1,693,942	963,304	131,547
1978/1979	580,880	1,626,386	1,074,286	146,293
1979/1980	391,990	1,550,323	1,150,372	200,288
1980/1981	277,003	1,468,538	1,177,813	205,000
1981/1982	342,700	1,409,800	1,182,600	200,000
1982/1983	392,900	1,363,100	1,116,900	200,000
1983/1984	393,700	1,283,000	1,140,900	222,200
1984/1985	N.A.	N.A.	N.A.	240,000

Sources: For adult, primary, and secondary education from 1970/1971 through 1980/1981, Ministerio de Educación, *Informe a la Asamblea Nacional del Poder Popular* (Havana: 1981), pp. 344–46; for 1981/1982 through 1983/1984, Ministerio de Educación, *Organización de la educación 1981-1983, informe a la XXXIX Conferencia Internacional de Educación, Ginebra, Suiza 1984* (Havana: 1984), p. 173. For higher education from 1970/1971 through 1979/1980, Ministerio de Educación, *Informe*, pp. 344–46; for 1980/1981, Elena Díaz González, "La mujer y necesidades humanas básicas," *Economía y Desarrollo* 64 (September-October 1981): 219; for 1981/1982 through 1983/1984, Ministerio de Educación, *Organización*, p. 173; for 1984/1985, Federación de Mujeres Cubanas, *Cuban Women in Higher Education* (Havana: Editorial Letras Cubanas, 1985), p. 22.

a. Includes all university-level day, evening, and correspondence courses.

Table 4.2

Primary, Secondary, and Higher Education Enrollments as a Percentage of Total Enrollments in Cuba, 1970/1971 and 1983/1984

School Year	Primary	Secondary	Higher	Total
1970/1971	83.3%	14.8%	1.9%	100%
1983/1984	48.5	43.1	8.4	100

Sources: Author's computations based, for 1970/1971, on Ministerio de Educación, *Informe a la Asamblea Nacional del Poder Popular* (Havana: 1981), pp. 344–47; for 1983/84, Ministerio de Educación, *Organización de la educación 1981-1983, informe a la XXXIX Conferencia Internacional de Educación, Ginebra, Suiza 1984* (Havana: 1984), p. 173.

Table 4.3

Percentage of Students' Retention in Various Types of Cuban Secondary Schools, 1970/1971 and 1982/1983

Type of School	1970/1971	1982/1983
Basic Secondary (Grades 7-9)	84.1%	94.2%
Preuniversity (Grades 10-12)	86.9	93.2
Polytechnical (Grades 7-13)	N.A.	87.7
Teacher Training (Grades 10-13)	72.8	92.5

Sources: For 1970/1971, Ministerio de Educación, *Informe a la Asamblea Nacional del Poder Popular* (Havana: 1981), p. 252; for 1982/1983, Ministerio de Educación, *Organización de la educación 1981–1983, informe a la XXXIX Conferencia Internacional de Educación, Ginebra, Suiza 1984* (Havana: 1984), p. 177.

Table 4.4
Cuban Higher Education Enrollments by Subject Area, 1969/1970 and 1979/1980

Subject Area	1969/1970	Enrollment 1979/1980	% Change
Agricultural Sciences	5,154	19,628	280.8%
Technology	7,948	36,252	356.1
Natural and Exact Sciences	3,420	8,813	157.7
Medical Sciences	7,977	23,033	188.7
Humanities, Social Sciences, and Art	2,178	12,618	479.3
Education	1,627	78,513	4,725.6
Economic Studies	1,214	21,431	1,665.2
Total	29,518	200,288	578.5%

Sources: For 1969/1970, Ministerio de Educación Superior, *Informe de la delegación de la Republica de Cuba a la VII Conferencia de Ministros de Educación Superior y Media Especializada de los Países Socialistas* (Havana, 1972), pp. 117–18. For 1979/1980, author's computations based on the total enrollment figures and the percent distribution of enrollment by "Specialty" (*Grupo de Especialidad*) given in Ministerio de Educación, *Informe a la Asamblea Nacional de Poder Popular* (Havana: 1981), pp. 346, 365. All percentage change figures computed by author.

Note: The total enrollment figure for 1969/1970 given in the first source above is somewhat lower than that given in the second and used in Table 3.1. The most likely reason for this discrepancy is that the first source may not include some categories of higher education enrollments, such as in correspondence courses. The first source is used here because it is the only one to categorize enrollment by "Faculty," here labeled "Subject Area." Until 1977, Cuban higher education was organized according to "Faculties," and thereafter according to "Specialties." See "Ley que establice la estructura de especializaciones para la educación superior," Universidad de la Habana 203/204 (1976):175–79. The second source provides no breakdown for 1969/1970, and categorizes 1979/1980 enrollments by "Specialty." In order to make the figures for the two years reported compatible, the author has had to judge which "Specialty" would have belonged to which "Faculty," if the latter were still the organizing principle in force; thus, there is some chance of error here, but probably not much.

Table 5.2
Estimated Change in Number of Cuban Refugee and Non-Refugee Secondary School Graduates, 1959-1980

	As of 1959	1959-1962	1963-1965	1966-1968	1969-1971	1972-1974	1975-1977	1978-1980
New Secondary School Graduates in Cuba	—	17,583	14,324	23,810	28,495	35,269	125,827	265,649
Refugee Labor Force Participants with Twelve or More Years of Schooling	—	31,519	9,512	21,010	18,466	2,942	1,398	10,505
Cumulative Total of Secondary School Graduates Remaining in Cuba	117,375	103,439	108,251	111,051	121,080	153,407	277,836	532,980

Sources: Top Line from Table 5.1.

Second Line estimated and computed by author from figures for refugee labor force participants in Table 2.2 and various estimates of how many of these had twelve or more years of schooling. For 1959 through 1965, an estimate of 36.0 percent was used, based on Richard Fagen, et al., *Cubans in Exile: Disaffection and Revolution* (Stanford: Stanford University Press, 1968), p. 19; for 1965 through 1971, an estimate of 37.0 percent was used, based on the 1968 study by Eleanor Rogg, *The Assimilation of Cuban Exiles* (New York: Aberdeen Press, 1974), as cited in Alejandro Portes, et al., "The New Wave: A Statistical Profile of Recent Cuban Exiles to the United States," *Cuban Studies/Estudios Cubanos*, 7, 1 (January 1977), p. 13; for 1972 through 1980, an estimate of 22.0 percent was used, based on data for 1973-1974 reported in Robert L. Bach, "The New Cuban Immigrants: Their Background and Prospects," in U.S. House of Representatives, Committee on the Judiciary, *Caribbean Migration*, Ninety-Sixth Congress: 1980, p. 312.

Third line estimated and computed by author. The 117,375 figure for 1959 is the author's estimate based on 1953 Census figure of 99,143, increased by 18.39 percent, the same percentage increase as the total population over this period. The rest of these figures computed by subtracting the second line from the top line and adding the result to the previous total for this third line.

Note: Since data for the number of refugee secondary school graduates are not available, it was necessary to use the closest approximation, "twelve or more years of schooling." The category of Refugee Labor Force Participants with Twelve or More Years of Schooling includes some individuals without secondary diplomas, since prior to the 1977/1978 academic year, Cuban students had to compete thirteen, not twelve, years of schooling to receive a secondary degree. See Ministerio de Educación, *Documentos directivas para el perfeccionamiento del Sistema Nacional de Educación* (Cuba: 1975), p. 35. Using the figures in this refugee category to compute the Cumulative Total of Secondary School Graduates Remaining in Cuba thus underestimates the number of secondary school graduates, the new professionals, left in the country. This underestimation is offset to some extent by two other factors that tend to overestimate the number of new professionals remaining in Cuba: First, these educational data do not make it possible to distinguish between new professionals and revolutionary leaders with comparable education. Second, no deduction for retirement and death has been made from these figures.

The alert reader will notice that using these educational data results in different estimates of the number of intermediate-level refugees in various years than did the occupational data used in Table 2.2. For 1959–1962, the educational data result in a lower estimate, probably because in prerevolutionary Cuba some incumbents of intermediate occupations possessed fewer than twelve years of schooling. For all other years, and in total, the educational data result in higher estimates. There are probably two reasons for this: First, as explained above, since thirteen years of schooling were needed to graduate before 1977/1978, the number of refugee secondary school graduates is lower than the number with only twelve years of schooling. Second, some individuals probably left the country after completing twelve or more years of schooling but before entering the labor force at the intermediate-level.

There is no way to combine occupational and educational data to arrive at a uniform estimate of intermediate-level refugee labor force participants. Therefore, since both types of data are useful for different purposes, and since the estimates derived from these two types of data do not differ inordinately, it seems better to present both.

Table 5.1 [*Table 5.2 appears on last two pages.*]
**Graduates of Secondary Schools in Cuba,
 1959/1960 to 1979/1980**

Year	Secondary School Graduates
1959/1960 – 1961/1962	17,583
1962/1963 – 1964/1965	14,324
1965/1966 – 1967/1968	23,810
1968/1969 – 1970/1971	28,495
1971/1972 – 1973/1974	35,269
1974/1975 – 1976/1977	125,827
1977/1978 – 1979/1980	265,649
Total	510,957

Source: Author's computations based on Ministerio de Educación, *Informe a
la Asamblea Nacional del Poder Popular* (Havana: 1981), pp. 421–25, 427.

Note: These include all graduates of preuniversities, of polytechnical
institutes at the medium-level technician grade, of secondary teacher education schools, and of secondary-level adult education schools, as well as
graduates of medium-level technician courses offered by organizations other
than the Ministry of Education.

Table 5.3

**Percentage of New Entrants to the University of Havana
 by Highest Educational Level of Parents, 1970/1971**

Highest Educational Level	Mother	Father
Not Specified	6%	8%
Primary (Grades 1–4)	60	49
Basic Secondary (Grades 5–9)	17	19
Advanced Secondary (Grades 10–13)	12	14
Higher Education	5	10
Total	100%	100%

Source: Ministerio de Educación, *Informe de la delegación de la Republica
de Cuba a la VII Conferencia de Ministros de Educación Superior y Media
Especializada de los Países Socialistas* (Havana: 1972), p. 52.

Table 5.4
Estimated Chance of 1953 Potential Fathers (Males aged 15–44) with Various Educational Backgrounds to Have Generated a Child Enrolled in Higher Education in 1970/1971

Father's Educational Background	Potential Fathers, 1953	Higher Education Students 1970/1971	Chance of Potential Fathers to have a Child in Higher Education
No Formal Education	321,736	—	—
Not Specified	—	2,811	0.87%
Primary (Grades 1-4)	923,132	17,217	1.87
Basic Secondary (Grades 5-9)	39,431	6,676	16.93
Advanced Secondary (Grades 10-13)	24,682	4,919	19.93
Higher Education	27,067	3,514	12.98
Total	1,336,048	35,137	2.63

Sources: "Potential fathers": author's computations based on 1953 *Censos de población.* "Higher education students": author's computations from estimates based on the assumption that the distribution of father's education for all students in higher education in 1970/1971, as given in Ministerio de Educación, *Informe a la Asamblea Nacional del Poder Popular* (1981), p. 345, was the same as for "new entrants to the University of Havana," as given in Table 5.3. Percentages in the third column: author's computations.

Table 5.5

Percentage of Women Among All Cuban Graduates of Medium-Level Technician and Higher Education, by Field of Study and Selected Age Groups, 1981

	Medium-Level Technician			Higher Education		
			Age Groups			
	20-24	40-49	All	20-24	40-49	All
Field of Study						
Geology, mining, metallurgy	22.9	11.5	0.7	50.0	12.1	28.5
Energy	23.8	6.2	13.4	26.0	7.2	11.9
Machine building	40.1	11.2	21.5	30.0	6.9	11.2
Sugar, chemical, & food industries	59.3	45.0	50.7	64.2	27.6	41.0
Electronics, automation, communications	33.4	19.8	22.1	25.0	9.6	18.0
Transportation	19.2	4.9	9.7	17.8	5.4	11.4
Construction	41.9	13.5	28.8	43.9	16.1	28.1
Agriculture, livestock	35.8	12.7	24.2	56.1	5.0	27.8
Economic studies	71.1	49.0	55.5	64.7	24.9	37.3
Public health, physical culture	74.2	64.3	75.0	51.3	31.3	40.3
Arts	80.5	62.6	67.4	47.2	40.8	41.7
Natural and exact sciences	—	—	—	57.9	53.3	52.8
Social sciences, humanities	—	—	—	56.7	32.8	41.1
Education	—	—	—	57.2	68.1	58.2
Other	45.2	33.4	37.7	52.5	37.2	46.0
All Fields	52.2	39.0	42.7	54.3	33.1	40.1

Source: Adapted from the analysis of the 1981 Cuban census by Isabel Larguia and John Dumoulin, "Women's Equality and the Cuban Revolution," in June Nash and Helen Safa, eds., *Women and Change in Latin America* (South Hadley, MA: Bergin & Garvey Publishers, 1986), p. 368.

INDEX

Administration: blamed for negative economic practices, 173; bureaucracy within, 142–43; Communist Party and, 66; Communist Party directive on, 174–75; evaluation and promotion mechanisms, 107; labor hoarding, 147; new principles following post-1970 rectification of, 73–74; removal from posts, 176; revolutionary examples within, 168; skill problem and bureaucracy and, 57–58; tension between workers and, 65; unions and, 78–79; wage rates and inefficiency in, 62–63; women in, 114. *See also* New professionals; Old cadres

Adult education programs, 44; enrollment following post-1970 rectification in, 90

Agriculture: absenteeism rates, 64; auto-finance system in, 52; Basic Units of Cooperative Production, 195–96; corruption and profiteering, 166; labor shortage, 194; move from sugar monoculture, 41; production growth, 133; specialization, 41–42; special period programs concerning, 193–97; work contingents in, 194–95; work- study programs, 121–26. *See also* Sugar

Allen, Richard, 4

Association of Third World Economists: Second Congress of, 117

Auto-finance system: in agriculture, 52

Banner of the Heroes of Moncada, 80

Basic Units of Cooperative Production (UBPC), 195–96

Batista, Fulgencio, 23, 46

Bay of Pigs invasion, 4

Biotechnology industry, 190

Black market, 198

Blockade. *See* Economic blockade

Bray, Donald, 36

Brundenius, Claes, 59, 133

Budget: deficit increase, 197, 199

Bukharin, Nikolai, 50

Bureaucracy, 53; "antibureaucratic revolution," 57; democratic centralism and, 75. *See also* Bureaucratic centralism

Bureaucratic centralism: as practiced by Castro, 135–36; catego-